I0438690

Peak Streamflows and Runoff Volumes for the Central United States, February through September, 2011

By Robert R. Holmes, Jr., Gregg J. Wiche, Todd A. Koenig, and Steven K. Sando

Professional Paper 1798–C

U.S. Department of the Interior
U.S. Geological Survey

U.S. Department of the Interior
SALLY JEWELL, Secretary

U.S. Geological Survey
Suzette M. Kimball, Acting Director

U.S. Geological Survey, Reston, Virginia: 2013

For more information on the USGS—the Federal source for science about the Earth, its natural and living resources, natural hazards, and the environment, visit http://www.usgs.gov or call 1–888–ASK–USGS.

For an overview of USGS information products, including maps, imagery, and publications, visit http://www.usgs.gov/pubprod

To order this and other USGS information products, visit http://store.usgs.gov

Suggested citation:
Holmes, R.R., Jr., Wiche, G.J., Koenig, T.A., and Sando, S.K., 2013, Peak streamflows and runoff volumes for the Central United States, February through September, 2011: U.S. Geological Survey Professional Paper 1798–C, 60 p., http://pubs.usgs.gov/pp/1798c/.

Contents

Figures

Tables

Conversion Factors

Inch/Pound to SI

Multiply	By	To obtain
Length		
inch (in.)	2.54	centimeter (cm)
inch (in.)	25.4	millimeter (mm)
foot (ft)	0.3048	meter (m)
mile (mi)	1.609	kilometer (km)
Area		
acre	4,047	square meter (m^2)
acre	0.4047	hectare (ha)
acre	0.4047	square hectometer (hm^2)
acre	0.004047	square kilometer (km^2)
square mile (mi^2)	259.0	hectare (ha)
square mile (mi^2)	2.590	square kilometer (km^2)
Volume		
acre-foot (acre-ft)	1,233	cubic meter (m^3)
acre-foot (acre-ft)	0.001233	cubic hectometer (hm^3)
Flow rate		
cubic foot per second (ft^3/s)	0.02832	cubic meter per second (m^3/s)

Horizontal coordinate information is referenced to the North American Datum of 1983 (NAD 83).

Water year is the 12-month period from October 1 to September 30 and is designated by the year in which it ends. For example, Water Year 2011 would be the 12-month period from October 1, 2010 to September 30, 2011.

Peak Streamflows and Runoff Volumes for the Central United States during the 2011 Floods

By Robert R. Holmes, Jr., Gregg J. Wiche, Todd A. Koenig, and Steven K. Sando

Abstract

During 2011, excessive precipitation resulted in widespread flooding in the Central United States with 33 fatalities and approximately $4.2 billion in damages reported in the Souris/Red River of the North (Souris/Red) and Mississippi River Basins. At different times, beginning in late February 2011 and extending through September 2011, various rivers in these basins had major flooding, with some locations receiving multiple rounds of flooding. Peak streamflow records were broken at 105 streamgages in the Souris/Red and Mississippi River Basins and annual runoff volume records set at 47 of the 211 streamgages analyzed for annual runoff. For the period of 1950 through 2011, the Ohio River provided almost one-half of the annual runoff at Vicksburg; the Missouri River contributed less than one-fourth, and the lower Mississippi River less than one-fourth. Those relative contribution patterns also occurred in 1973 and 2011, with the notable exception of the decrease in contribution of the lower Mississippi River tributaries and the increase in contribution from the upper Missouri River Basin in 2011 as compared to 1973 and the long-term average from 1950 to 2011.

Introduction

Major flooding in parts of the upper Mississippi River, Missouri River, Ohio River, middle and lower Mississippi River, Red River of the North (Red River), which includes the Souris River, in the Central United States (fig. 1) and the southern Prairie Provinces of Canada at various times during 2011, caused 33 fatalities and approximately $4.2 billion (B) in damages (National Oceanic and Atmospheric Administration, 2011a). The flooding began in earnest in February and March in parts of the lower Missouri River, middle and lower Mississippi River, and Ohio River Basins. Snowmelt flooding began in late March and early April in the Red River and upper Mississippi River Basins, followed by successive flooding in the lower Mississippi River, and Missouri River Basins (second round) from mid-April through August. The Souris River, a part of the Red River of the North Basin, experienced a second round of flooding in June 2011. The 2011 floods in the Central United States were caused by one or more combinations of the following: saturated soil conditions, higher than average streamflow headed into 2011, rapid melting of the larger than normal snowpack, excessive precipitation on snowpack, or simply excessive precipitation. In some parts of the Central United States, precipitation amounts in excess of 20 inches in a 2-week period (700- to 1,000-percent above normal) were observed (National Oceanic and Atmospheric Administration, 2012a) following snowpack greater than 150 percent of normal in parts of the northern U.S. Rocky Mountains (Rockies) (National Oceanic and Atmospheric Administration, 2012b). During the 2011 flooding, the U.S. Geological Survey (USGS) made more than 2,300 direct measurements of streamflow at USGS streamgages and other strategic river locations to enable documentation of peak streamflows, stages, and runoff volumes at locations throughout the Central United States.

Purpose and Scope

Throughout the United States, the USGS operates a network of more than 7,800 streamgages, providing data that are vital to human, economic, and environmental welfare. As the principal federal agency charged with the mission of documenting the water resources of the United States and assisting with understanding of natural hazards, it is important to document floods, particularly those of epic proportions. USGS streamflow data, some existing back to the late 1800s, are important to place context to magnitudes of the 2011 floods. This report documents the peak streamflow and runoff volumes at selected locations in the Central United States during 2011.

Mississippi River levee along the Louisiana State University campus in Baton Rouge, Louisiana on May 21, 2011. Photograph by Zach Martin, USGS.

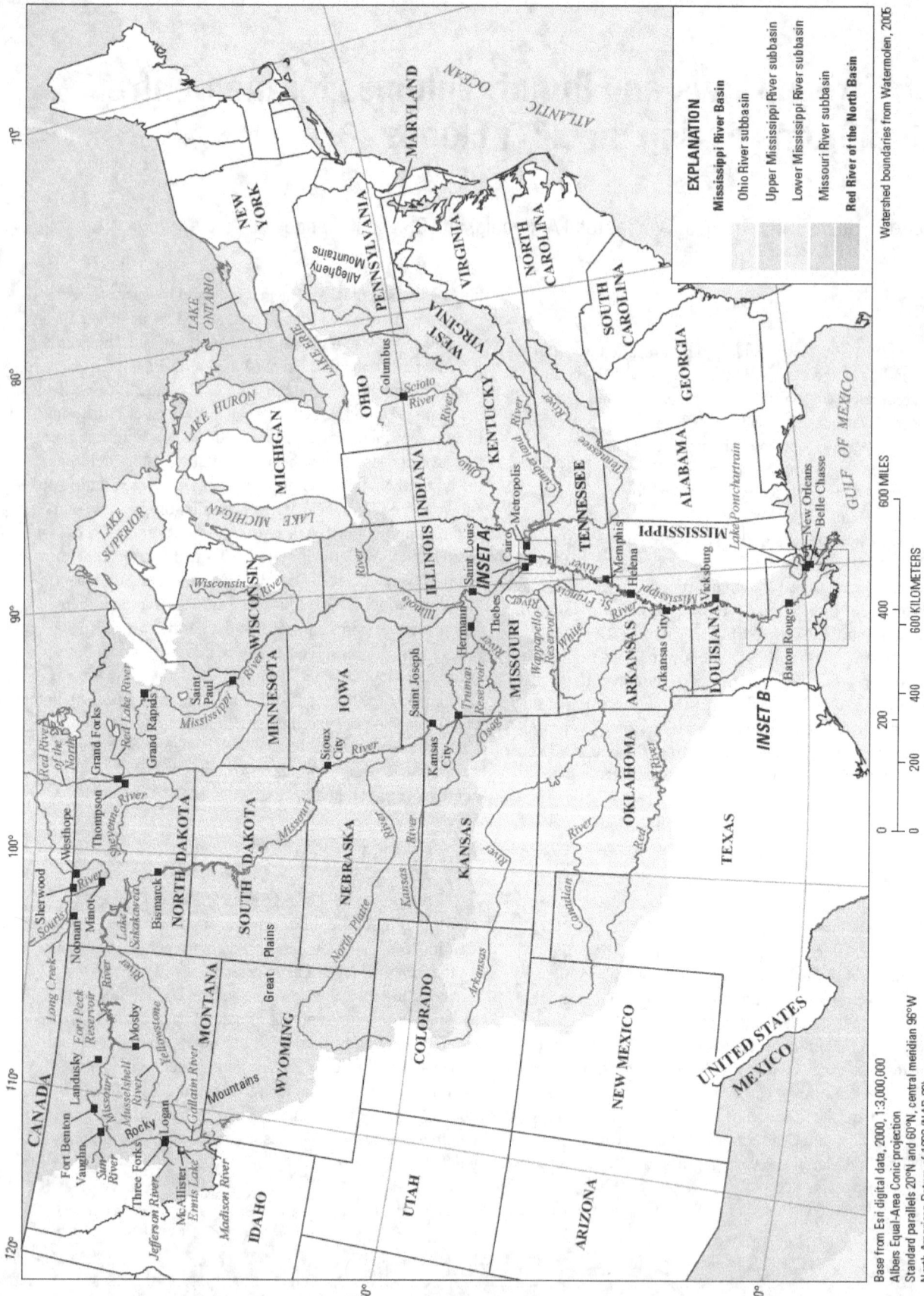

Figure 1. Major river basins of the Central United States along with other locations affected by flooding streams from February to September, 2011.

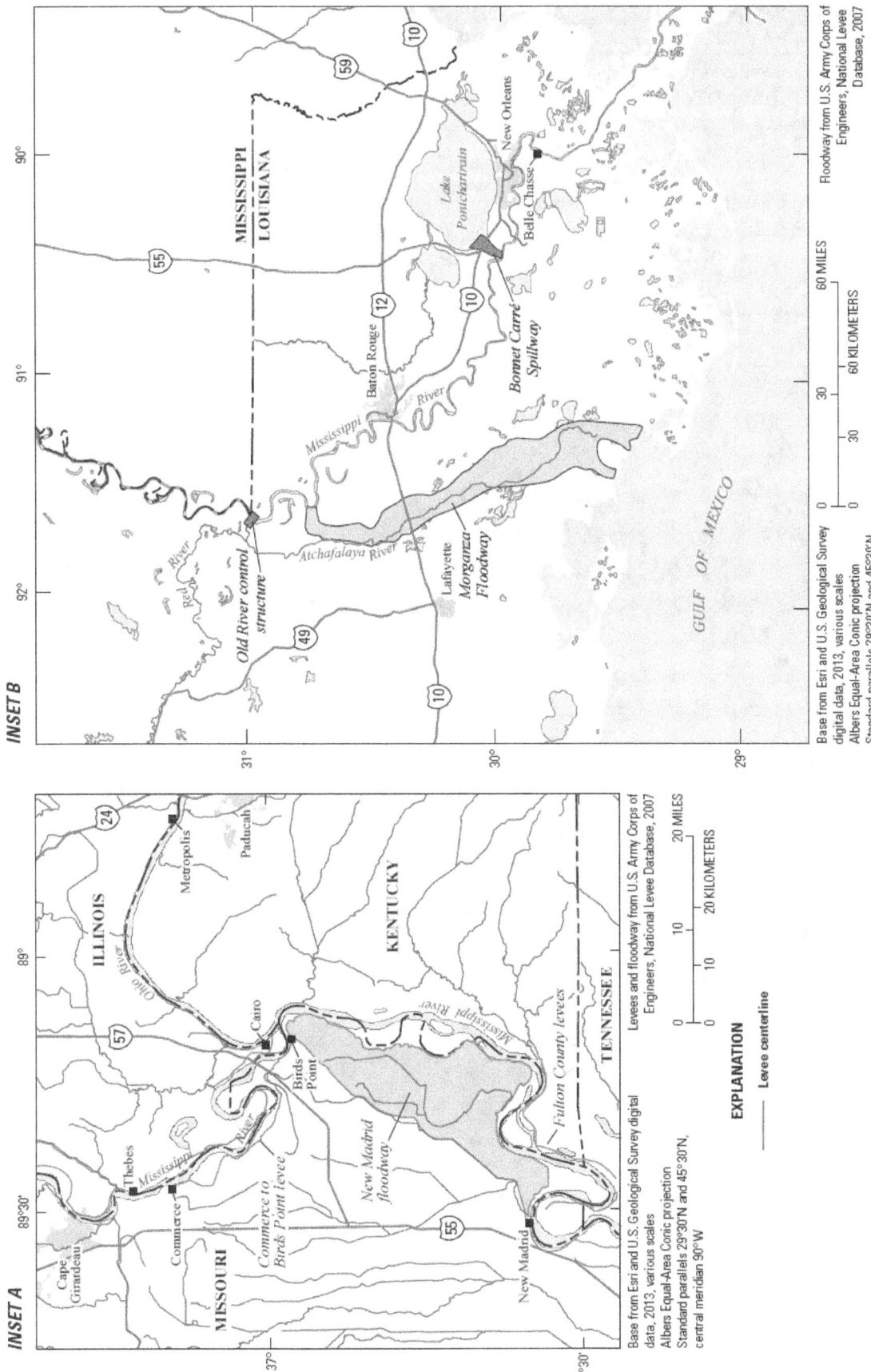

Base from Esri and U.S. Geological Survey digital
data, 2013, various scales
Albers Equal-Area Conic projection
Standard parallels 29°30'N and 45°30'N,
central meridian 90°W

Levees and floodway from U.S. Army Corps of
Engineers, National Levee Database, 2007

EXPLANATION

——— Levee centerline

Base from Esri and U.S. Geological Survey
digital data, 2013, various scales
Albers Equal-Area Conic projection
Standard parallels 29°30'N and 45°30'N,
central meridian 90°W

Floodway from U.S. Army Corps of
Engineers, National Levee
Database, 2007

Figure 1. Major river basins of the Central United States along with other locations affected by flooding streams from February to September, 2011.—Continued

Chronology of 2011 Flooding

The effects of the La Niña climate pattern (Vining and others, 2013) on the late summer and fall 2010 precipitation across the Northern Plains and upper Midwest left the soils saturated (National Oceanic and Atmospheric Administration, 2011a) and many rivers and streams flowing at above-normal levels (fig. 2) going into the winter freeze up. By late winter 2010–2011, the below-normal temperatures and above-normal precipitation resulted in a large snowpack (National Oceanic and Atmospheric Administration, 2011b). Depending on the river basin in the Central United States, the dominant causes

of flooding were excessive rainfall, rapidly melting snowpack, or both. Many river basins had more than one round of flooding in 2011.

The first episodes of flooding during 2011 in the Central United States began in late February and early March in parts of the lower Missouri, middle and lower Mississippi, and Ohio River Basins, all stemming from excessive rainfall. Numerous streamgages had stages above flood stage after widespread rain of as much as 6 inches fell between February 20 and March 1 in parts of these basins (National Weather Service, 2012). The cumulative effect of this first round of flooding is illustrated by selected stage hydrographs for the main-stem upper and lower Mississippi, Ohio, and Missouri Rivers near

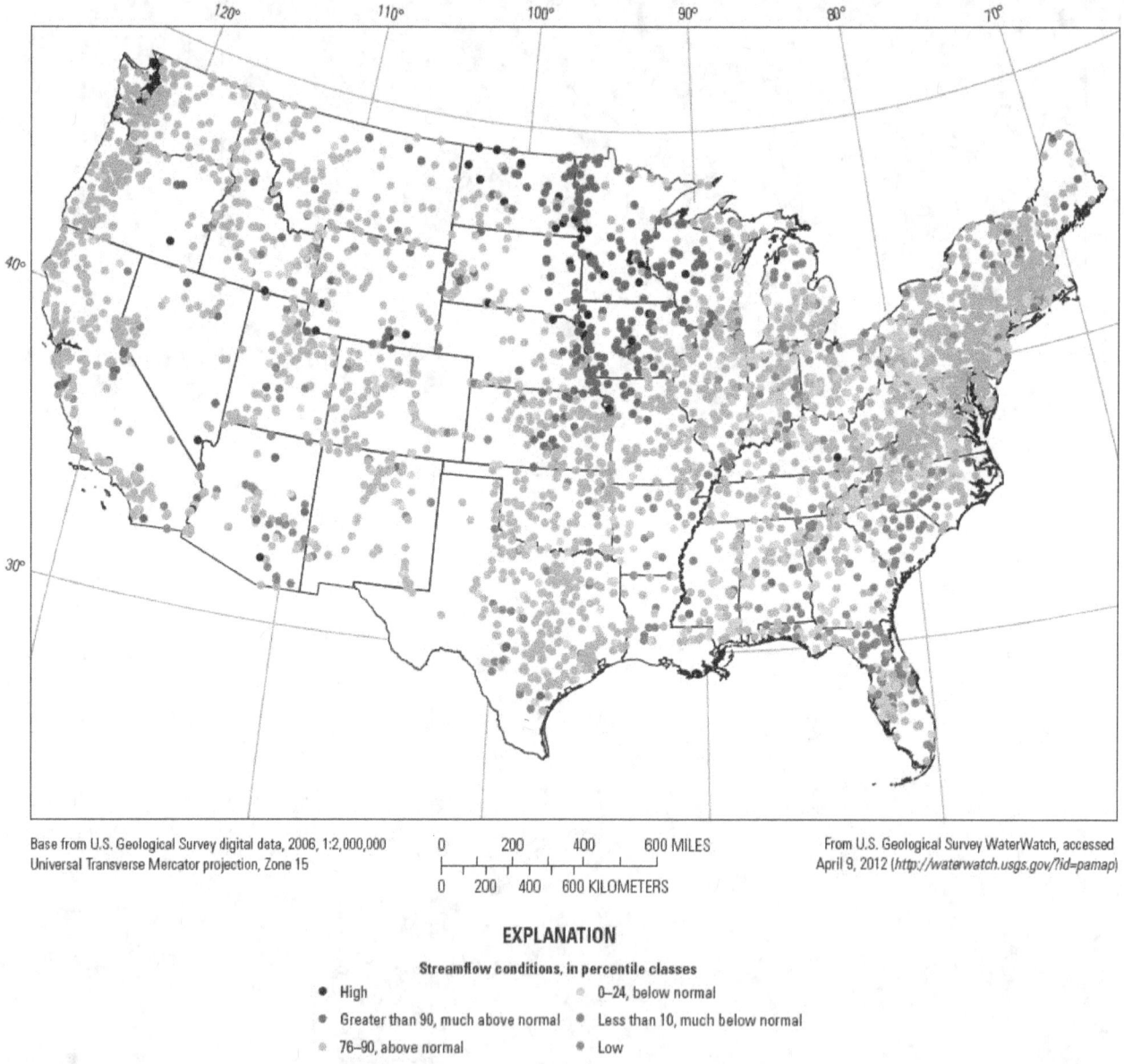

Base from U.S. Geological Survey digital data, 2006, 1:2,000,000
Universal Transverse Mercator projection, Zone 15

From U.S. Geological Survey WaterWatch, accessed April 9, 2012 (*http://waterwatch.usgs.gov/?id=pamap*)

EXPLANATION

Streamflow conditions, in percentile classes

- High
- Greater than 90, much above normal
- 76–90, above normal
- 25–75, normal
- 0–24, below normal
- Less than 10, much below normal
- Low

Figure 2. Streamflow conditions at U.S. Geological Survey streamgages on November 15, 2010 (U.S. Geological Survey, 2012a).

the end of February and the beginning of March (fig. 3). The February/March round of flooding was the first of three flood waves to move through the reach of the Mississippi River downstream from St. Louis (fig. 3A). As flood waves move downstream, they often attenuate, with a general broadening and elongation of the flood hydrograph. Evidence of attenuation is particularly evident in the April–June flooding on the Mississippi River (fig. 3A).

Rising temperatures in March in the upper Midwest and Northern Plains were accompanied by additional rainfall. Rivers in the northern reaches of the upper Mississippi River Basin and Red River of the North Basin began to flood in mid-March and into April. The low gradient of the Red River of the North and its tributary streams resulted in flooding of long duration compared to similarly sized river basins elsewhere in the United States. During the 2011 flood, the Red River at Grand Forks, N. Dak. (USGS streamgage 05082500) was above flood stage for 52 days, cresting on April 14 (table 1, at the back of the report) and not falling below flood stage until May 20, 2011. Some initial flooding during March and April in the Souris River Basin in Canada and the United States lacked the severity that would come later in the summer of 2011. The upper Mississippi River tributaries in the northern part of the basin crested in late March and early April, sending a second flood pulse down the upper Mississippi River (fig. 3A). Downstream tributaries to the upper Mississippi River, particularly the Illinois and Missouri Rivers, contributed large streamflows that were the result of the 6 to 15 inches of rainfall that fell over parts of the upper Mississippi Basin during the month of April (Vining and others, 2013).

The Missouri River upstream from Sioux City, Iowa is regulated by a series of six large multiuse main-stem dams constructed between 1933 and 1963 to "be operated for the purposes of flood control, navigation, irrigation, power, water supply, water quality control, recreation, and fish and wildlife" (U.S. Army Corps of Engineers, 2006). The total system storage for the six main-stem reservoirs operated by the U.S. Army Corps of Engineers (USACE) is 73.1 million acre-feet (MAF) (U.S. Army Corps of Engineers, 2012a). The main-stem reservoirs were drawn down to a total system storage of 56.8 MAF (which is the base of the annual flood control pool; as a result all 2010 floodwaters had been evacuated (Kevin Grode, U.S. Army Corps of Engineers, written commun., Nov. 19, 2012) by January 28, 2011, to provide approximately 16.3 MAF of flood control storage (U.S. Army Corps of Engineers, 2012b). The plains snowpack in the upper Missouri River Basin started to melt in mid-February and by April 1, 2011, total available flood control storage decreased to about 7.6 MAF (U.S. Army Corps of Engineers, 2012b). During the May rainfall, and on through July, much of the remaining storage in the six main-stem reservoirs on the Missouri River was used in an attempt to decrease flood elevations on the Missouri River (U.S. Army Corps of Engineers, 2012c). Although the Missouri River reservoirs are not operated to reduce flooding on the Mississippi River, by reducing flooding on the Missouri

River, this typically has a secondary effect of reducing the flooding (even though slight) on the Mississippi River. Other flood control reservoirs in the Missouri and Mississippi River Basins, such as the Harry S. Truman Reservoir in central Missouri (U.S. Army Corps of Engineers, 2012b) and Wappapello Reservoir in southeast Missouri (Camillo, 2012, p. 70 and p. 105) held flood water back that decreased the peak streamflows downstream on the Mississippi River.

The Ohio River Basin, particularly the lower end of the Ohio River Basin, received as much as 15 to 20 inches of rainfall during April (Vining and others, 2013), sending a second flood pulse down the main stem of the Ohio River (fig. 3B). Flood control reservoirs in the Tennessee and Cumberland River Basins (tributaries to the Ohio River) were used, when many of these reservoirs were already at record or near record levels, in an attempt to hold back as much water as possible from the Ohio River in an effort to decrease the flood crest in the area of the confluence of the Ohio and Mississippi Rivers (Camillo, 2012, p. 63–70, p. 98). The second flood crest of the season of the Ohio River arrived at the confluence with the Mississippi River at Cairo, Ill. (confluence area) just as the second upper Mississippi River flood pulse was cresting at Thebes, Ill. (USGS Streamgage 07022000) in late April (figs. 3A and 3B). These two flood crests proceeding down the respective rivers also were coincident with a large multi-day rainfall event from April 24 to May 3 (National Weather Service, 2012) centered over the confluence area, extending in area for hundreds of miles, and producing almost daily rainfalls (except April 29 and April 30) in excess of 3 inches in parts of the confluence area.

As the flood waves combined and flowed into the lower Mississippi River, the U.S. Army Corps of Engineers (USACE) activated the New Madrid Floodway (NMFW) at 10 p.m. local time on May 2 for only the second time in history (Camillo, 2012, p. 116–118). NMFW was activated to lessen water levels upstream on the flood wall at Cairo, Ill. and the Commerce-Birds Point levee, along with the Fulton County levees paralleling the NMFW across the river in Kentucky (Camillo, 2012, p. 33, p. 71, p. 76). The flood crest moved down the lower Mississippi River enhanced by floodwaters from the St. Francis, White, and Arkansas Rivers in Arkansas. The crest arrived at Memphis, Tenn. (USACE streamgage 07032000) on May 9 and 10, and at Arkansas City, Ark. (USACE streamgage 07265450), and Vicksburg, Miss. (USGS streamgage 07289000) on May 17. Because of complicated hydraulics of large river systems, such as the Mississippi River, the streamflow can peak before the stage crest, by as much as a day or more, and often can peak along a large reach (on the order of a 100 miles) of the river in the same day, as was the case on the lower Mississippi River during the 2011 flood.

Flooding in the lower Mississippi River Basin below Arkansas City, Ark. was virtually nonexistent during much of 2011 outside of what was occurring on the main-stem Mississippi and Atchafalaya Rivers and small stream flooding in the State of Mississippi from early spring thunderstorms.

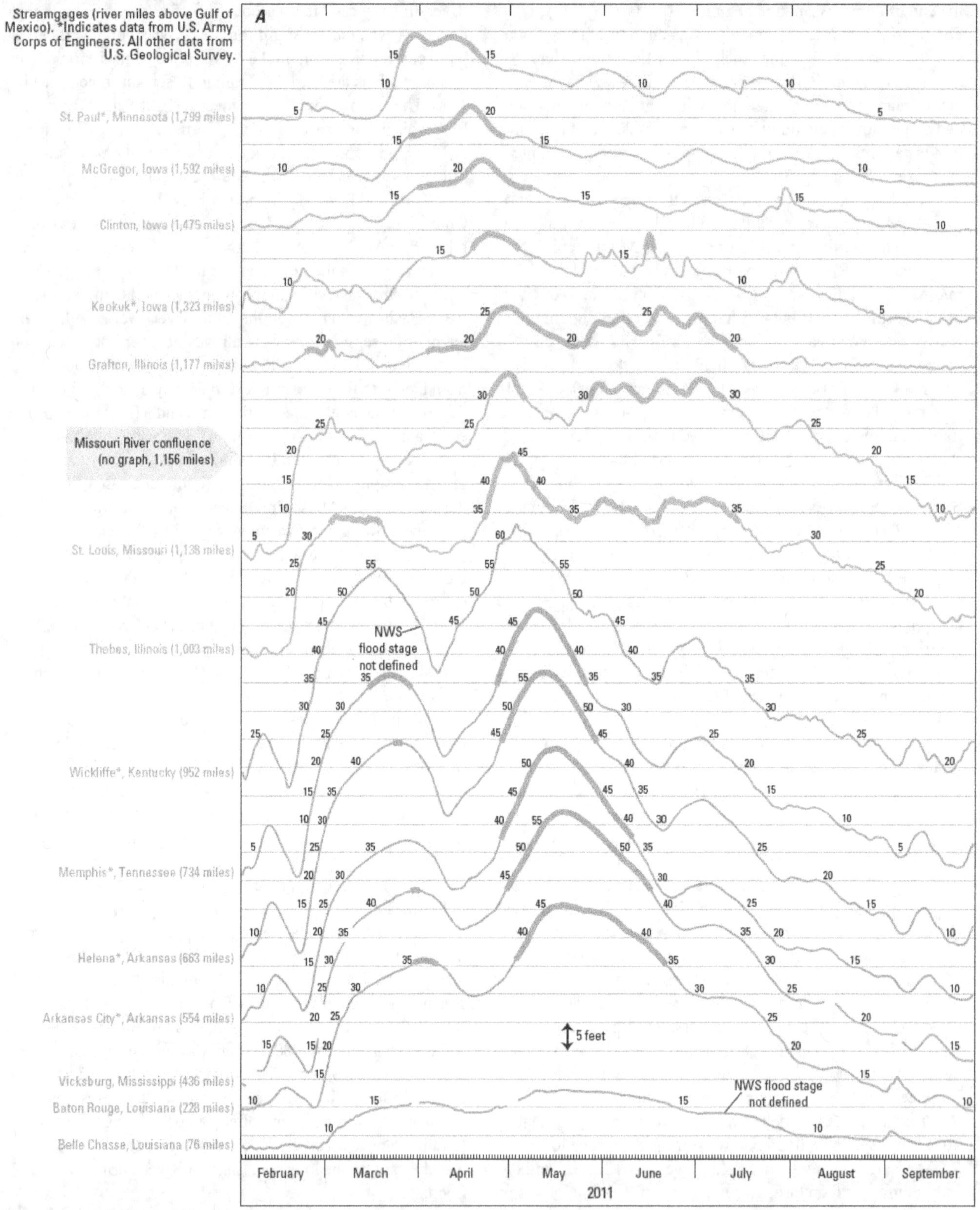

Figure 3. Stage hydrographs of selected streamgages on the *A*, upper and lower Mississippi Rivers (U.S. Geological Survey, 2011; Mark Richter, U.S. Army Corps of Engineers, Memphis District, written commun., May 29, 2012; Thomas Nock, U.S. Army Corps of Engineers, Rock Island District, written commun., May 30, 2012).

EXPLANATION

Streamgages—Numbers above line indicate gage height, in feet, at each streamgage. Bold line segments indicate gage heights exceeding National Weather Service (NWS) flood stage, if defined for that streamgage

Upper Mississippi River (above the confluence with the Ohio River)

Lower Mississippi River (below the confluence with the Ohio River)

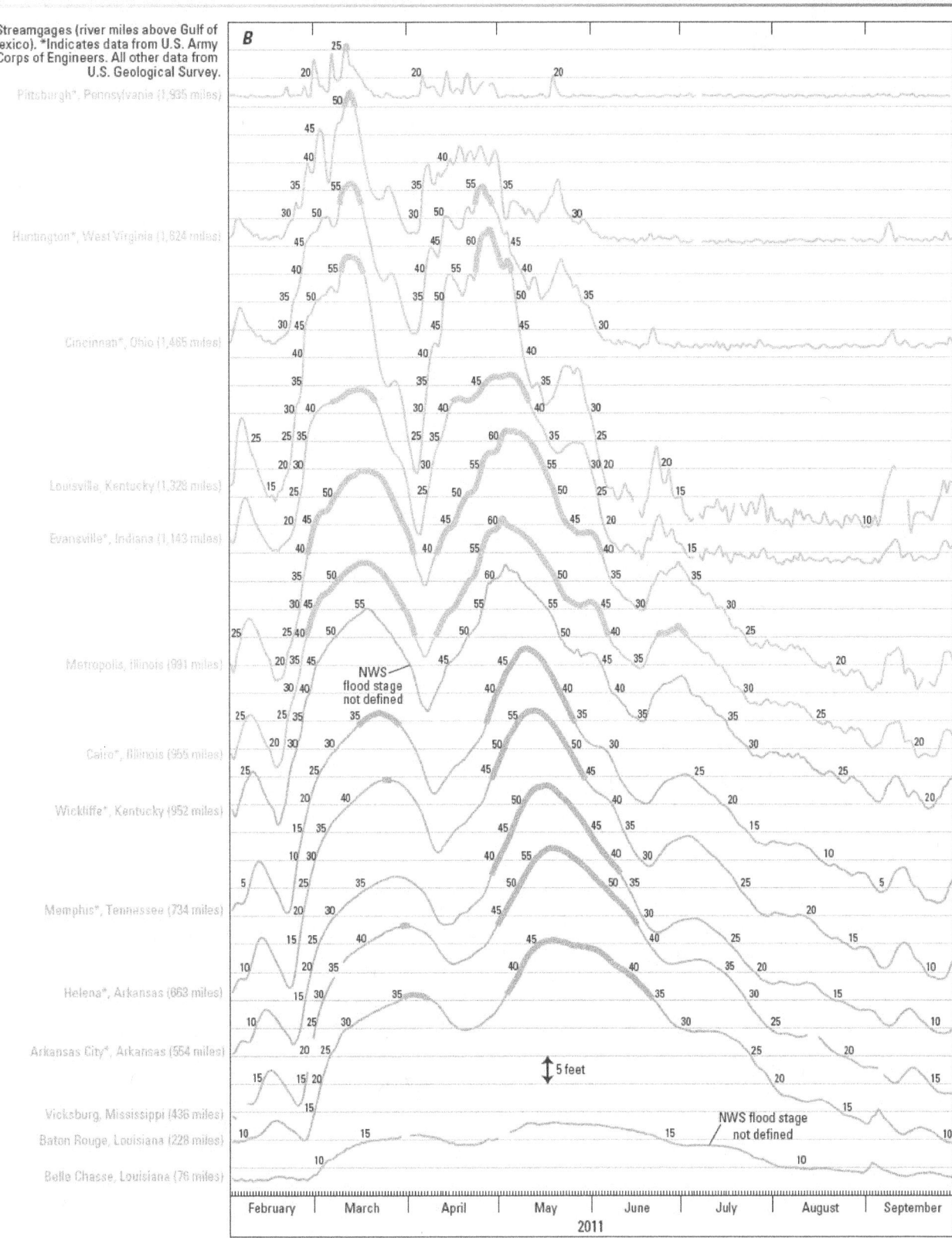

Figure 3. Stage hydrographs of selected streamgages on the *B*, Ohio and lower Mississippi Rivers (U.S. Geological Survey, 2011; Robert Moyer, U.S. Army Corps of Engineers, Ohio River Division, written commun., July 26, 2012; Mark Richter, U.S. Army Corps of Engineers, Memphis District, written commun., May 29, 2012).—Continued

EXPLANATION

Streamgages—Numbers above line indicate gage height, in feet, at each streamgage. Bold line segments indicate gage heights exceeding National Weather Service (NWS) flood stage, if defined for that streamgage

Ohio River

Lower Mississippi River (below the confluence with the Ohio River)

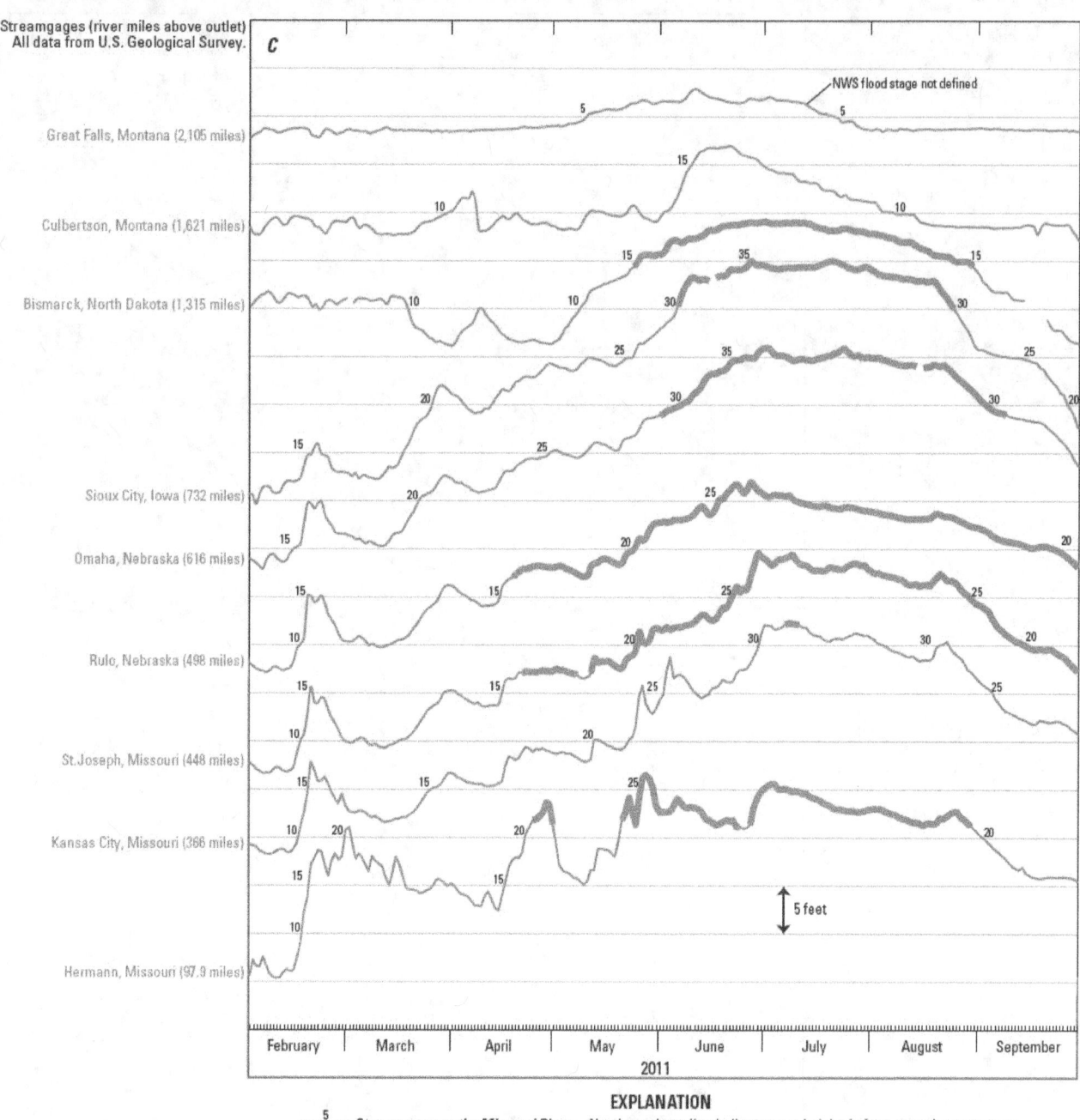

Figure 3.   Stage hydrographs of selected streamgages on the *C,* Missouri River from February to September 2011 (U.S. Geological Survey).—Continued

Streamflow was much below normal in many of the tributary rivers in the southern extent of the lower Mississippi River Basin (U.S. Geological Survey, 2012b).

Approximately 119 miles downstream from Vicksburg, Miss., the flow of the Mississippi River is partially diverted into the Atchafalaya River at all times of the year through the Old River Control Structure (Old River), with the purpose of maintaining the distribution of the upstream flow at 70 percent continuing down the Mississippi River and 30 percent diverted into the Atchafalaya (Camillo, 2012, p. 13). During the 2011 flood, a maximum value of 671,000 cubic feet per second (ft³/s) was diverted through the Old River and into the Atchafalaya River at the peak of the flood (Camillo, 2012, p. 278). Downstream of Old River, the USACE activated the Morganza Floodway (Morganza) for only the second time since it was completed in 1954 to bypass additional flow into the Atchafalaya River from the Mississippi River to prevent flooding downstream at Baton Rouge, La. and farther downstream. A maximum of 195,000 ft³/s was diverted through Morganza during the height of the flooding (Paul Ensminger, USGS Louisiana Water Science Center, written commun., Sept. 18, 2012). Finally, to protect New Orleans, La. and other locations, the Bonnet Carré Spillway (Bonnet Carré) was activated to bypass water from the Mississippi River into Lake Pontchartrain, with a maximum diversion of 314,000 ft³/s on May 19, 2011 (Paul Ensminger, USGS Louisiana Water Science Center, written commun., Sept. 14, 2012). The 2011 flood was the first time that NMFW, Morganza, and Bonnet Carré floodways were operated simultaneously.

With the diversions of water at Old River, Morganza, and Bonnet Carré, the peak streamflow of the Mississippi River was decreased by almost 1 million ft³/s from Vicksburg, Mississippi (USGS streamgage 07289000) to Belle Chasse, La. (USGS streamgage 07374525), before emptying in the Gulf of Mexico, with the difference flowing to the Gulf of Mexico either by way of the Atchafalaya River system or Lake Pontchartrain. Given the unusual hydraulics of the lower Mississippi River below Vicksburg, induced by the various flow diversion control structures (Old River, Morganza, and Bonnet Carré), the Mississippi River at Belle Chasse crested on May 17, concurrent with the crest at Vicksburg, and a day earlier than the crest upstream at Baton Rouge, Louisiana (USGS streamgage 07374000).

While the lower Mississippi River was cresting and beginning to recede in mid- to late-May, the combination of widespread snowmelt and prolonged, heavy rainfall in the Rockies and Great Plains was producing major flooding on the upper Missouri River. May 2011 saw as much as 15 to 20 inches of rain in parts of the Missouri River basin (National Weather Service, 2012). Rainfall totals during late May and early June in parts of Montana approached or exceeded average annual rainfall of about 15 to 20 inches (National Oceanic and Atmospheric Administration, 2012b). The previously available flood control storage of the Missouri River main-stem reservoirs was substantially diminished from

the floodwaters in April and early May. The ensuing rainfall in late May and June, in addition to the snowmelt, resulted in 98 percent of the flood control storage in the main-stem reservoir being used at the peak amount of storage of flood water on July 1, 2011 (U.S. Army Corps of Engineers, 2012c). Hydrographs for many of the Missouri River streamgages (fig. 3C) are prolonged and drawn out, particularly on the downstream extent of the Missouri River, because of various factors including prolonged snowmelt, prolonged rainfall, and attenuation of the flood waves attributable to main-stem and tributary reservoirs.

The same meteorological patterns affecting the Missouri River Basin in May and June also affected the Souris River Basin with a second round of flooding, this time much larger than the first major flood in April. Snowmelt in March, causing rivers and reservoirs to be full, combined with heavy May and June rainfall, resulted in a record flood crest progressing down the Souris River, peaking upstream of Minot (USGS streamgage 05117500) and Westhope, N. Dak. (USGS streamgage 05124000) on June 25 and July 5, respectively. As is the case in the Red River of the North, the Souris Basin is low gradient and as such the flooding was prolonged. An example of the long flood duration is demonstrated by the Souris River at Minot, which was above flood stage for 131 days during this time.

Peak Streamflows and Stages

Peak streamflow and stage during the 2011 floods for 369 streamgages in the Upper Mississippi, Arkansas-Red-White, Ohio, Missouri, lower Mississippi, and Red-Souris River Basins are listed in table 1 (at the back of this report), with their locations shown in figure 4. The streamgages included in table 1 were chosen either because the 2011 peak streamflow for that site had an annual exceedance probability estimated to be less than 10 percent or were included to allow comparison with past major floods. The annual exceedance probability for the peak streamflows is documented in a separate chapter of this Professional Paper (Jerad Bales, USGS Water Missin Area, written commun., Nov. 2, 2011).

The rank for the 2011 streamflow peak at selected streamgages for the period of record are presented in table 1; 105 streamgages had peaks of record for streamflow. Because of engineering controls and manmade changes to the river and associated hydraulic controls, some locations that did not have record streamflow did experience record stage. Similarly, some streamgages experienced record streamflow but not record stage. Streamgages that had flood peak streamflows that were either peak of record, one of the top five peaks for that site, or had stages that were above National Weather Service (NWS) flood stage for the central United States are shown in figure 5.

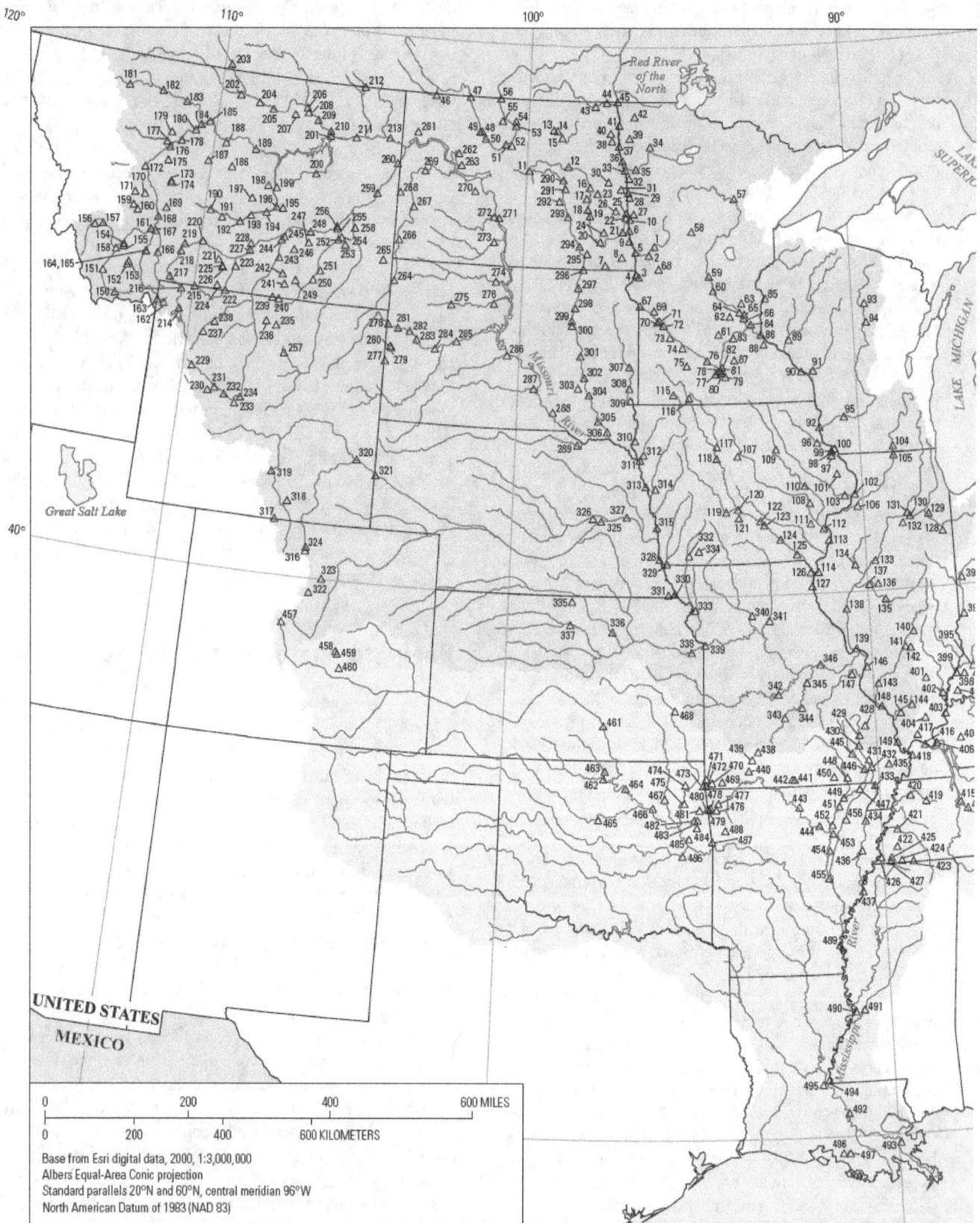

Figure 4. Locations of selected streamgages in the Central United States where flooding took place during the February to September, 2011.

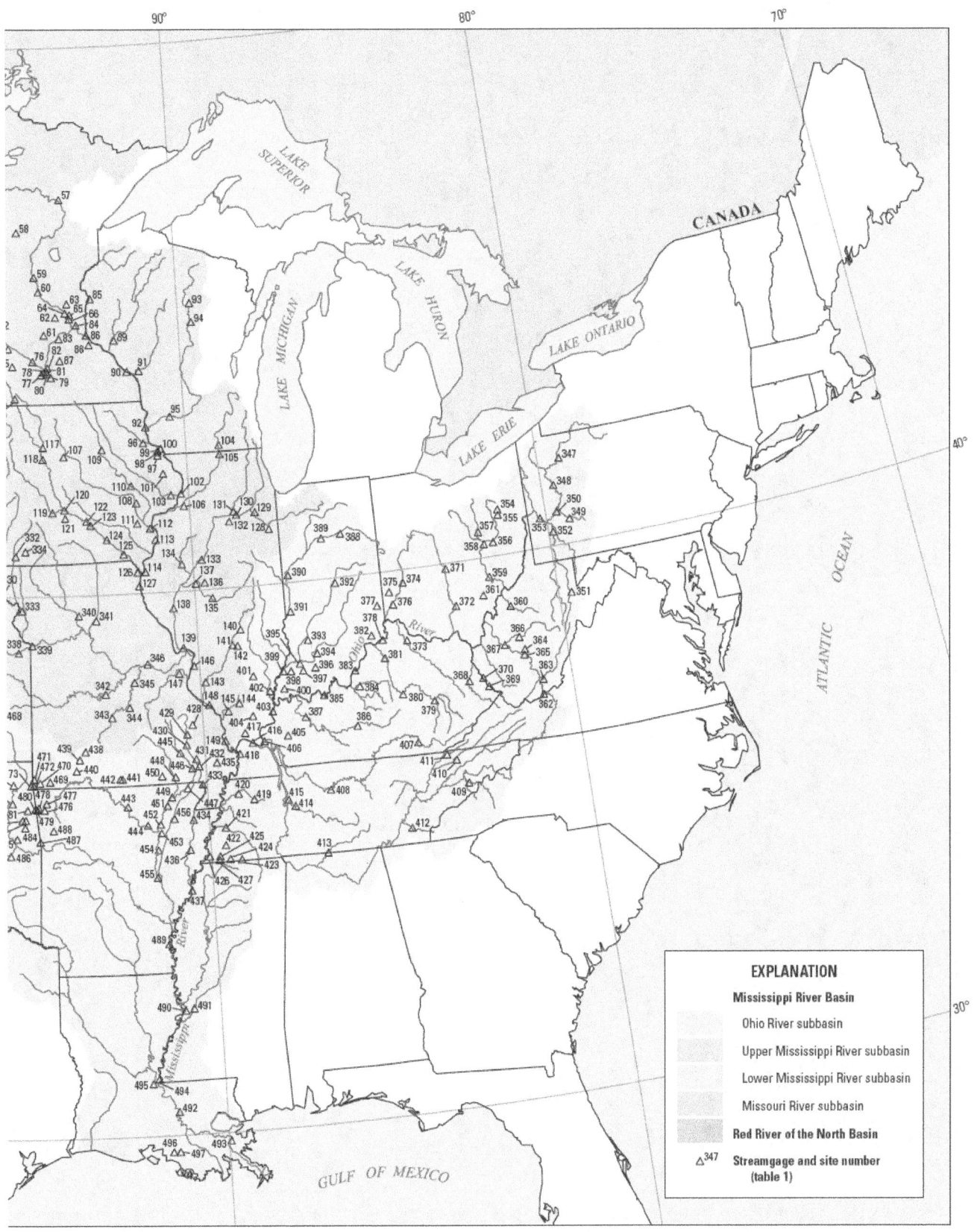

Figure 4.   Locations of selected streamgages in the Central United States where flooding took place during the February to September, 2011.—Continued

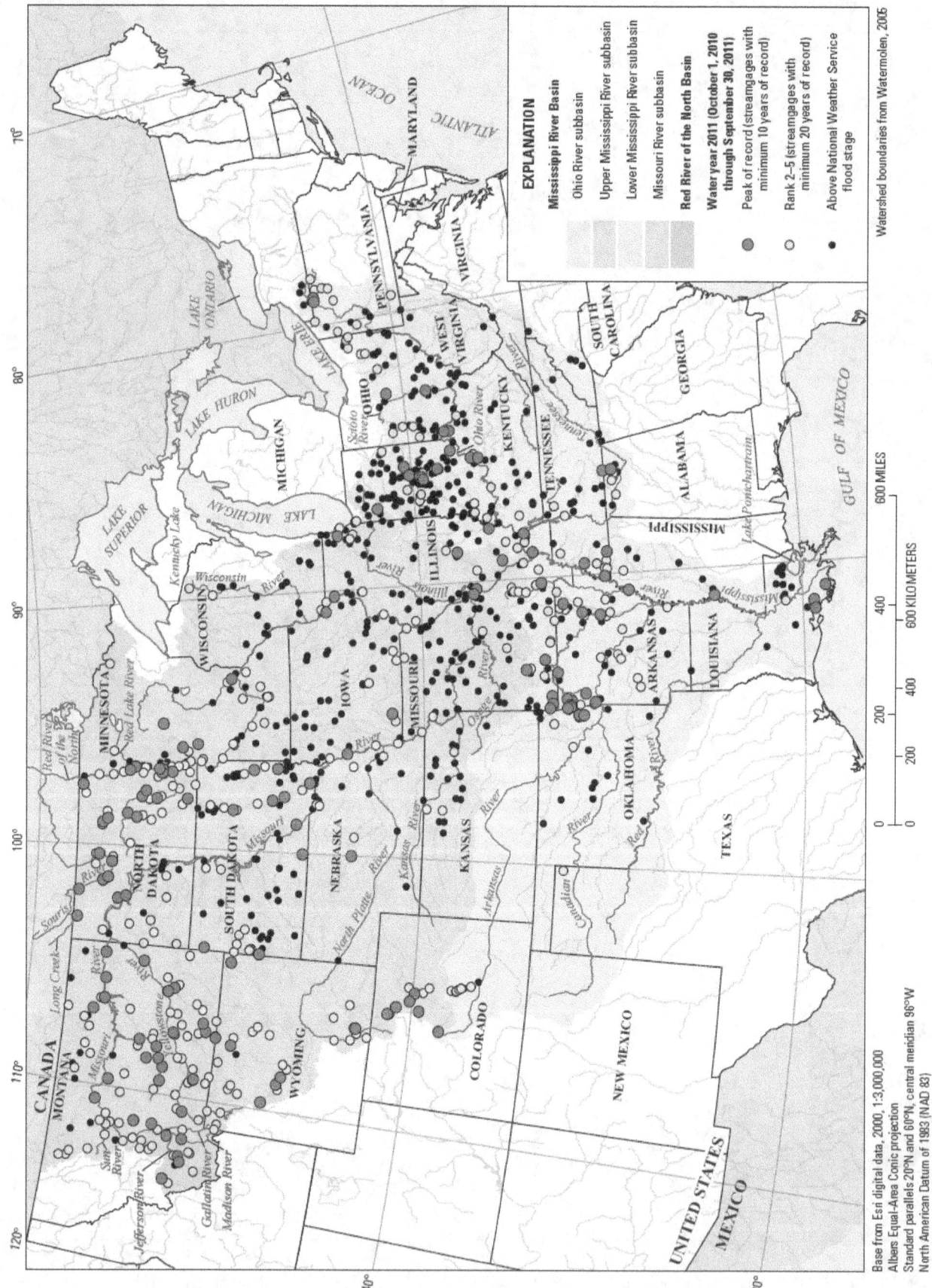

Figure 5.   Major flood peaks during 2011 in the central United States.

When comparing peak streamflow among stream locations and basins, the magnitude of streamflow must be considered in the context of the drainage area of the basin at that location. The Mississippi River at St. Louis, Mo. (USGS streamgage 07010000, table 1) 2011 peak streamflow of 615,000 ft³/s is large in comparison with the 26,900 ft³/s Souris River above Minot, N. Dak. (USGS streamgage 05117500, table 1). However, the Mississippi River at St. Louis drains 697,000 square miles (mi²) and the Souris River above Minot drains 3,900 mi². As a result, the peak yield of water for Minot was almost 8 times that at St. Louis (6.9 ft³/s/mi² compared to 0.88 ft³/s/mi²). The peak stream-flows along the Souris River were remarkable as they were the largest floods experienced by residents there in more than a century and caused an estimated $1 billion in damage (Win-nipeg Free Press, 2011). The peak streamflow at the Minot streamgage was the largest in 108 years of record and was more than twice as large as the next largest peak (table 1).

Although the flooding was major along many rivers and caused record peak streamflows at some locations in the Mississippi River Basin, many locations did not experience peak of record flooding. The more telling aspect of the 2011 floods was the vast spatial extent of major flooding across the Central United States. The flooding in the Missouri, upper Mississippi, and Ohio River Basins, although not the peak streamflow of record in all locations combined to cause record peak streamflow along reaches of the lower Mississippi River (table 1). These record peak streamflows along reaches of the lower Mississippi River are particularly remarkable given the long period of record for many of these Mississippi River streamgages and the history of the flood of 1927, which held the record in most of these locations until 2011. In addition, many flood control reservoirs and diversions, such as the Morganza and Bonnet Carré floodways, have been built since 1927. Without these structures, the peak streamflows in the lower Mississippi River would likely have been even larger.

Runoff Volumes

Runoff is that part of the precipitation, snowmelt, or irrigation water that appears in surface streams. It is gener-ally described in units of inches of water that would have uniformly covered a drainage basin or in units of acre-feet: the uniform depth of water in feet of water per acre that would result in the amount of runoff measured at a given loca-tion on a stream. Annual runoff volumes (annual runoff) for 211 streamgages in the Souris and Red River of the North, Missouri, upper and middle Mississippi, Ohio, and lower Mississippi River Basins are listed in table 2 (at the back of this report). The 211 streamgages were selected with the overarching goal of analyzing the annual runoff volume of all the major subbasins in the Mississippi and Red River Basins, along with the main stem streamgages along the Mississippi, Missouri, Ohio, Red, and Souris Rivers. To increase the

contextual validity of the analysis, an attempt was made to use only streamgages with at least 50 years of record, although some exceptions were made. Of the 211 streamgages listed, 47 streamgages set new records for annual runoff in 2011. Of the 47 streamgages, none were in the lower Mississippi or Ohio River Basins (table 2).

In addition to the record peak streamflow described earlier, the maximum annual runoff for the period of record was recorded at all USGS streamgages in the Souris River Basin (fig. 6 and table 2). Based on the Souris River above Minot, N. Dak. streamgage data (USGS streamgage 05117500 with 108 years of record) and anecdotal accounts, the 2011 annual runoff was the greatest since N. Dak. statehood in 1889. Statistics of annual runoff for Long Creek near Noonan (USGS streamgage 05113600, table 2) provide insight into the magnitude of the 2011 flood. The total volume of water that flowed past the Noonan streamgage during the period from 1960 through 2010 was 1,448,000 acre-feet (acre-ft), and the annual runoff in 2011 was 390,200 acre-ft. As a result, the annual runoff for 2011 was equal to about 27 percent of all the runoff recorded in the previous 51 years of record.

Although a record peak streamflow along the Red River of the North was recorded only for the streamgage near Thompson, N. Dak. (USGS streamgage 05070000, table 1), with only 13 years of record, record annual runoff was recorded at all Red River of the North main-stem streamgages in the United States (table 2) and Canada (Robert Harrison, Manager, Surface Water Management, Manitoba Water Stew-ardship, oral commun., 2012). The Red River of the North near Thompson, N. Dak. does not appear in table 2 given its short period of record (13 years). The ratio of the 2011 runoff to the previous maximum annual runoff indicates the largest ratios (approximately 1.50) in the tributaries draining much of southeast North Dakota. Tributaries downstream from the confluence of the Red Lake River and Red River did not have record annual runoff, but generally ranked in the top five for the period of record (fig. 6 and table 2).

The Missouri River main stem begins in Montana at the confluence of the Jefferson, Madison, and Gallatin Rivers (fig. 7). The USGS streamgages for the Jefferson River near Three Forks, Mont. (USGS streamgage 06036650), Madison River below Ennis Lake near McCallister, Mont. (USGS streamgage 06041000), and Gallatin River at Logan, Mont. (USGS streamgage 06052500) received runoff in 2011 with rank values of 4, 19, and 6 respectively, for their periods of record (fig. 7 and table 2). Although the 2011 annual runoff volumes are not record volumes at these three streamgages, their combined volumes along with that of the sixth-ranked Sun River near Vaughn, Mont. (table 2, USGS streamgage 0608900) and other tributary contributions produced the maximum annual runoff for the 121-year period of record into the Missouri River at Fort Benton, Mont. (table 2, USGS streamgage 06090800). In addition to the record runoff into the Missouri River upstream from Fort Benton, record runoff from the high plains of Montana entered the Missouri River downstream from Fort Benton, and combined with

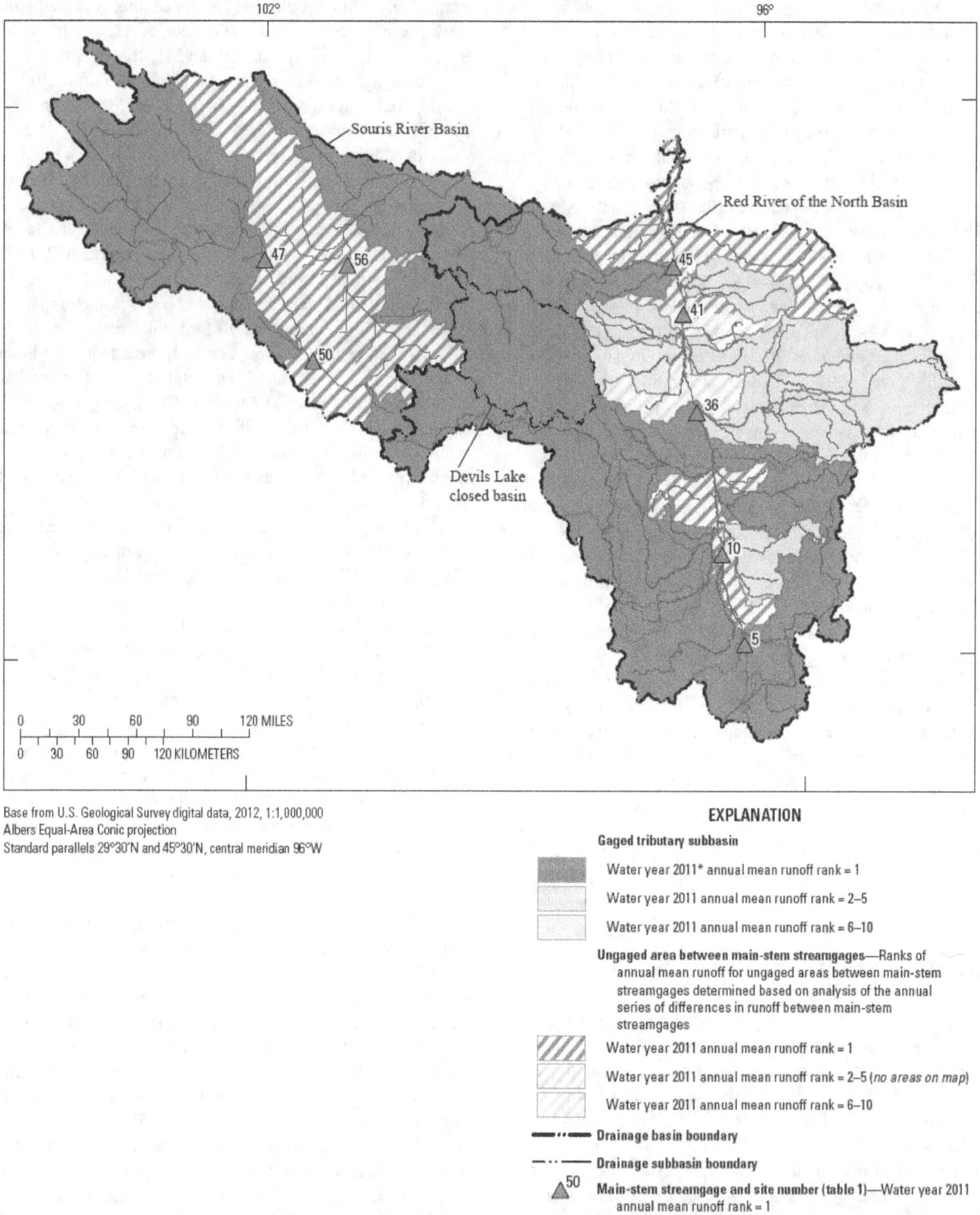

Figure 6. Ranks of the 2011 annual runoff for subbasins in the Souris/Red River of the North Basins for the 2011 water year.

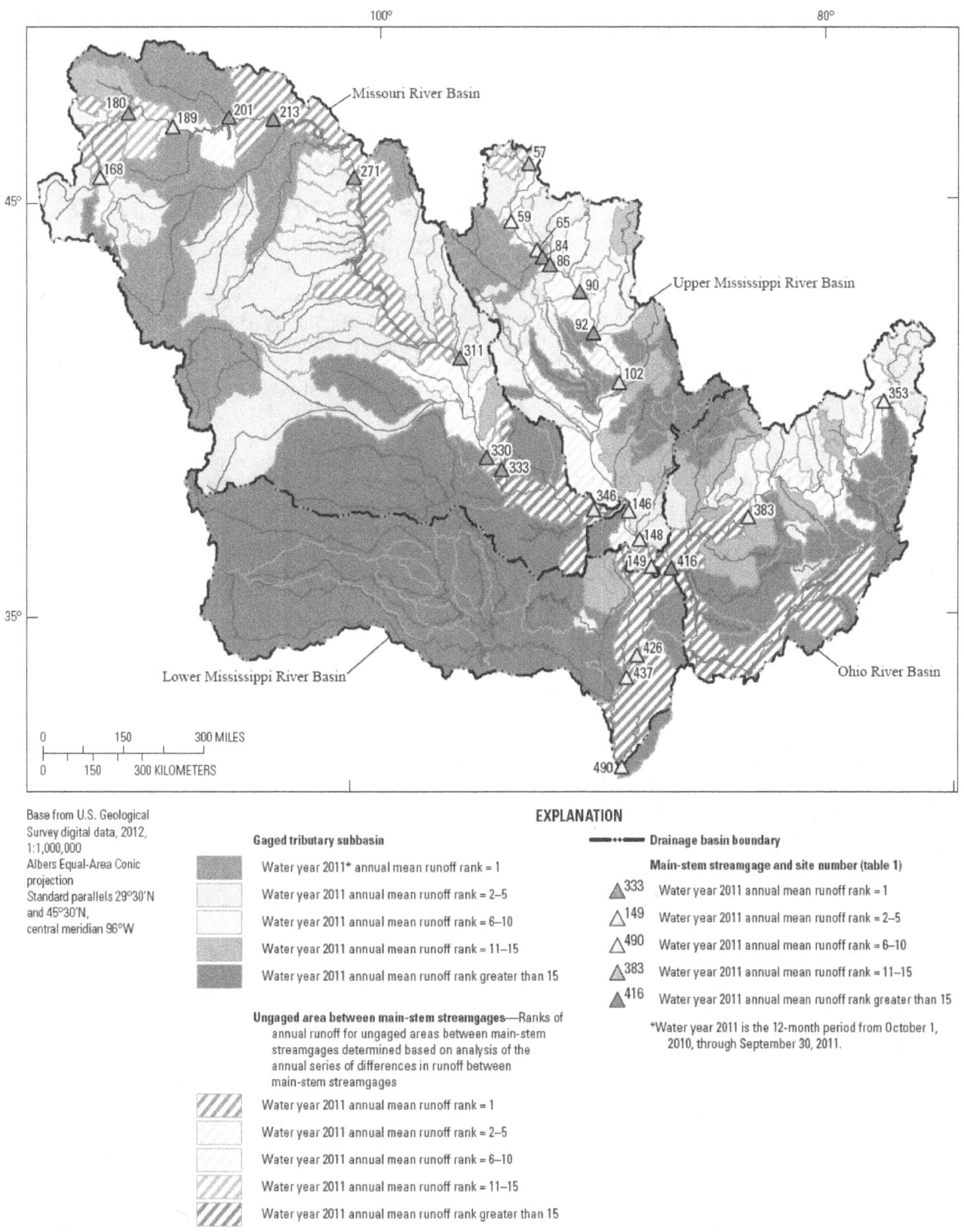

Figure 7.   Ranks of the 2011 annual runoff for subbasins in the Mississippi River Basins for the 2011 water year.

additional headwaters runoff from the Yellowstone River to produce record annual runoff at every main-stem streamgage on the Missouri River from Fort Benton (USGS Streamgage 06090800) to the Missouri River at St. Joseph, Mo. (USGS streamgage 06818000) except for the Missouri River near Landusky, Mont. (USGS streamgage 06115200), which ranked number two for the period of record (table 2).

Annual runoff from Missouri River tributaries draining large parts of North Dakota, South Dakota, northeast Wyoming, and northern Nebraska generally ranked from 1–5 for the period of record (fig. 7 and table 2). The four listed tributaries to the Missouri River downstream from St. Joseph, Missouri ranked in the range of 21 through 55 for 2011, with 3 of the 4 tributaries having runoff volumes below the mean annual runoff for the period of record. This illustrates that the flooding along the Missouri River was driven by the tributaries in the Rockies and Great Plains, with smaller contributions from the tributaries in Kansas, Iowa, and Missouri that made the 1993 flooding rank as the largest flood on the lower Missouri River (Parret and others, 1993; and Southard, 1995).

Much above normal annual runoff from the headwaters of the Mississippi River (upstream from Mississippi River at Grand Rapids, Minn., USGS streamgage 05211000), combined with record or near-record runoff from central and southern Minnesota tributaries to the Mississippi River (fig. 7 and table 2), produced the largest annual runoff (by a factor of 1.24) for the Mississippi River at St. Paul (USGS streamgage 05331000) for the 112-year period of record. Runoff from tributaries to the Mississippi River draining eastern Iowa and most of Illinois were above normal, but not peaks of record (table 2).

The 2011 annual runoff from many subbasins of the Ohio River Basin was above normal. As an example, annual runoff for the Ohio River at Metropolis, Ill. (USGS streamgage 03611500) ranked 26 out of 83 years of record (table 2), and the runoff was about 16 percent greater than the median annual runoff. As indicated by the rank of annual runoff listed in table 2, tributaries draining parts of western Pennsylvania, much of Ohio, and northern Kentucky had the largest comparative runoff in the Ohio River Basin, with ranks ranging from 2–12 for the period of record. An example tributary is the Scioto River at Columbus, Ohio (USGS streamgage 03227500) whose 2011 annual runoff ranked second (table 2). The cumulative runoff at this streamgage is shown in figure 8. Annual runoff into tributaries draining much of Kentucky, Indiana, and the southeastern part of Illinois were substantially above the median annual runoff, but well below record annual runoff. Annual runoff to the Ohio River from tributaries draining most of western West Virginia and Tennessee were slightly below to slightly above the median annual runoff for the respective stations (table 2).

Annual runoff from the Missouri River and the Mississippi Rivers upstream from St. Louis combined to produce the fifth largest annual runoff in 149 years of record on the Mississippi River at St. Louis, Mo. (USGS streamgage 07010000, table 2). Annual runoff from the large tributaries (Ohio and

White Rivers) entering the Mississippi River downstream from St. Louis was slightly above the median runoff, but runoff from the Arkansas River was much below the median annual runoff. The annual runoff for the Mississippi River at Vicksburg, Miss. (USGS streamgage 07289000) had the rank of 10 in 80 years of record.

Comparisons to Past Floods by Peak Streamflow and Runoff Volume

When comparing past floods, no single past flood is common to the entirety of the Central United States because the area is so large. However, the 2011 floods covered a vast area of the United States, with record or near-record peak streamflows (fig. 5) and annual runoff or both (figs. 6 and 7) occurring at streamgages near the Canadian border in the north to the headwaters of the Rockies in the west to the Allegheny Mountains in the east to New Orleans in the south.

The year of occurrence of the previous record flood is quite variable throughout the Central United States. This is not just by major basin (Red River, Missouri River, Ohio, upper Mississippi, and lower Mississippi River basins) but also within individual subbasins. The previous flood of record for peak streamflow at each streamgage is listed in table 1 and information for previous record runoff volumes is listed in table 2.

During 2011, the flooding resulted in a peak of record streamflow and a record annual runoff volume at every main-stem streamgage on the Souris River in Canada (Robert Harrison, Manager, Surface Water Management, Manitoba Water Stewardship, oral commun., 2012) and the United States (table 1 and 2). The 2011 flood far surpassed the previous flood of record in 1976 for peak streamflow and maximum annual runoff. Of particular note are the peak streamflows and runoff volumes recorded for 2011 along the Souris River. The 2011 runoff at Minot (1,969,000 acre-ft) was almost 2.5 times greater than the previous record annual runoff in 1976 (table 2). The 2011 annual runoff volume was 14 percent of the total runoff volume for the 108 years of recorded streamflow at this location.

For the 2011 flood in the Red River of the North Basin, only one location had record peak streamflow. For the most part, the 1997 and 2009 Red River of the North floods remain the largest peak streamflow at most locations. However, new records for annual runoff were set on many tributaries in the headwaters and at all main-stem streamgages on the Red River of the North in the United States (table 2) and Canada (Robert Harrison, Manager, Surface Water Management, Manitoba Water Stewardship, oral commun., 2012).

For a major river with long flow length, the year that the peak of record streamflow occurs may be different depending on the location along the river. For example, the 1993 flood is the peak of record streamflow for the lower Missouri River (Kansas City, Mo. to the mouth of the Missouri River), whereas in the middle parts of the Missouri River (Bismarck, N. Dak. to St. Joseph, Mo.), the 1952 flood, when Ft. Peck Dam was the only main-stem Missouri River dam in place, is the flood of record (fig. 9). The main-stem Missouri River dams have had a substantial impact in reducing peak streamflow in the middle reaches of the Missouri River. From table 1, the 2011 flood on the Missouri River main stem had peak of record streamflows at only three streamgages in Montana (table 1), which are at the upper end of the Missouri River.

Although few record peak streamflows were recorded during 2011 on the Missouri River main stem, several annual runoff records were recorded. The previous record annual runoff volume had been recorded in 1894 for the Missouri River at Fort Benton, Mont.; in 1975 for the main-stem Missouri River streamgages in the reach of the Missouri River from Landusky, Mont. to above Sioux City, Iowa; and in 1997 for those main-stem Missouri River streamgages from Sioux City, Iowa to St. Joseph, Mo.. The 2011 runoff volumes for the Missouri River at Hermann, Mo. (USGS streamgage 06934500) ranked fifth, with the peak of record annual runoff occurring in 1993. Some annual runoff volumes from tributaries to the Missouri River also set records for annual runoff. As an example, the 2011 runoff for the Musselshell River at Mosby, Mont. (fig. 8, USGS streamgage 06130500) was almost 11 times the median annual runoff and is nearly double the previous peak annual runoff in 1978 (table 2).

In contrast to the Mississippi and Missouri Rivers, no USGS Ohio River main-stem streamgage with more than 20 years of record had a peak of record during 2011. This is particularly notable because the Ohio River contributed the

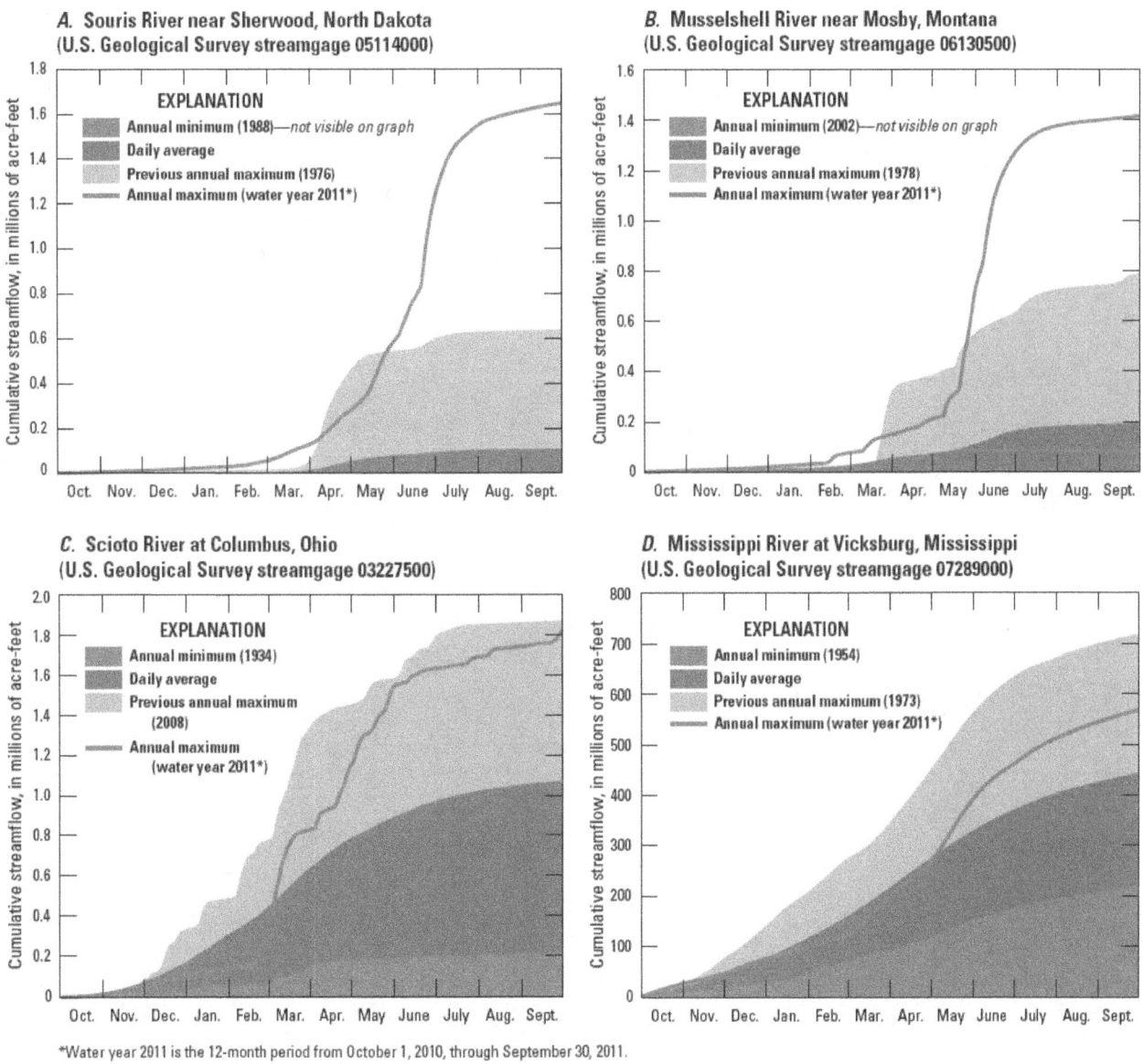

*Water year 2011 is the 12-month period from October 1, 2010, through September 30, 2011.

Figure 8.   Cumulative runoff for selected streamgages in the Central United States for the 2011 water year.

largest volume of flood water to the lower Mississippi River. However, without the retention of water by the flood control reservoirs in the Ohio River Basin, particularly along the Tennessee and Cumberland Rivers, it is conceivable that peak of record streamflows would have occurred in 2011. For the long-term main stem Ohio River streamgages, the 1937 flood is the flood of record in regards to peak streamflow (table 1). For annual runoff volume, 1979 and 2004 stand out as record years for the main-stem Ohio River (table 2).

The record peak streamflow for the Mississippi River is quite variable depending on location (table 1 and fig. 10).

Some of the large floods on the Mississippi River include those in 1844, 1912, 1927, 1937, 1945, 1965, 1993, and 2010. Peak streamflow records were set by the 2011 flood at the streamgages at Memphis, Tenn. (USACE streamgage 07032000), Helena, Ark. (USACE streamgage 07047970), Vicksburg, Miss. (USGS streamgage 07289000), and Belle Chasse, La. (USGS streamgage 07374525), all on the lower Mississippi River, although the streamgage at Belle Chasse has only 3 years of record. The 1927 flood on the Mississippi River inundated approximately 16.8 million acres from Cairo, Ill. to the Gulf of Mexico (fig. 11). The damages inflicted by

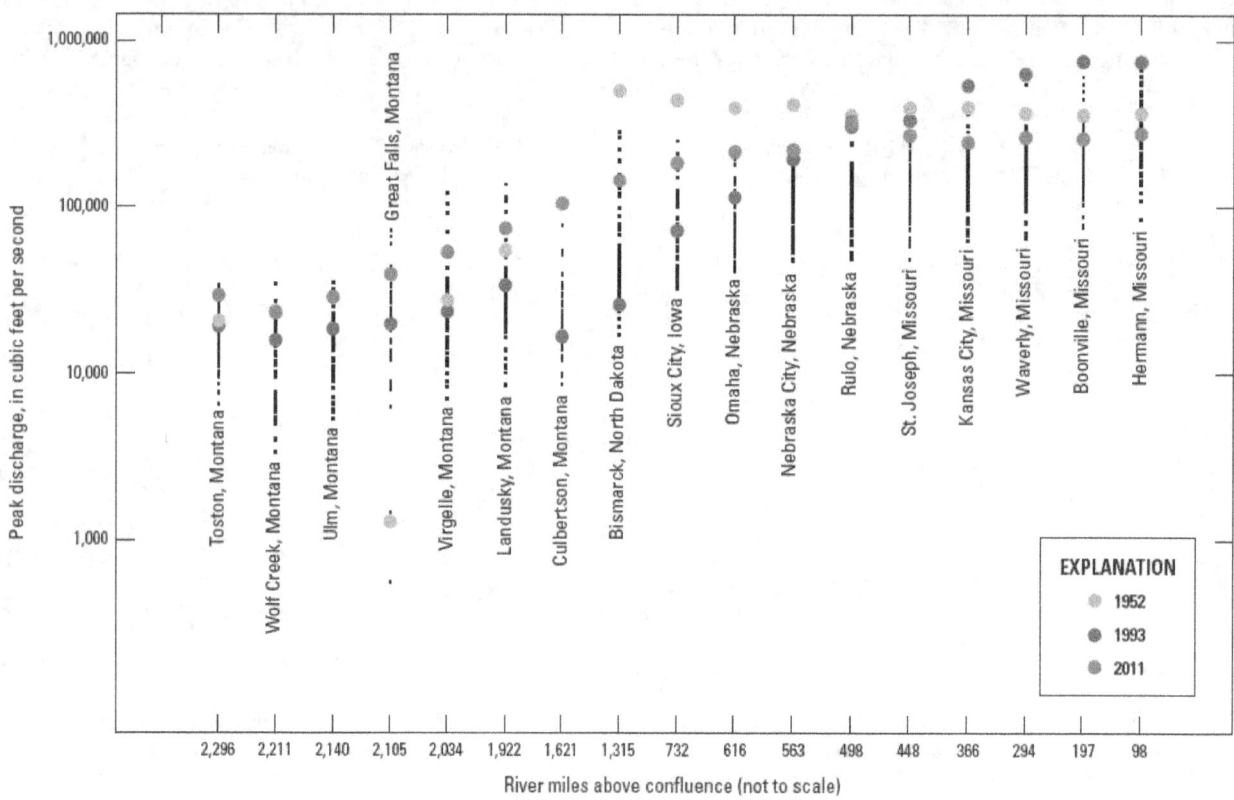

Figure 9.   2011 flood peaks on the Missouri River in relation to other selected floods.

Temporary U.S. Geological Survey streamgage installed downstream from the Morganza Floodway Control Structure , May 22, 2011. Photograph by Robert Holmes, USGS.

the 1927 flood resulted in establishment and construction of the Mississippi Rivers and Tributaries Project on the lower Mississippi River with the purpose of lessening flood effects to lands adjacent to the Mississippi River. The 2011 flood, with peak streamflows larger than those in 1927 at many locations, inundated only one-third of the land (approximately 5.16 million acres) that was inundated in 1927 (approximately 16.8 million acres) (fig. 11).

The record annual runoff for the Mississippi River at Vicksburg, Miss. (USGS streamgage 07289000) is 720.4 MAF in 1973, with the 2011 annual runoff volume ranking 10th

at 568.3 MAF (fig. 12 and table 2). For the period of 1950 through 2011, the Ohio River provided almost one-half of the annual runoff at Vicksburg, the Missouri River contributed less than one-fourth and the lower Mississippi River less than one-fourth (fig. 12). Those relative contribution patterns also occurred in 1973 and 2011, with the notable exception of the decrease in contribution of the lower Mississippi River tributaries and the increase in contribution from the upper Missouri River Basin in 2011 as compared to 1973 and the long-term average from 1950 to 2011 (fig. 12).

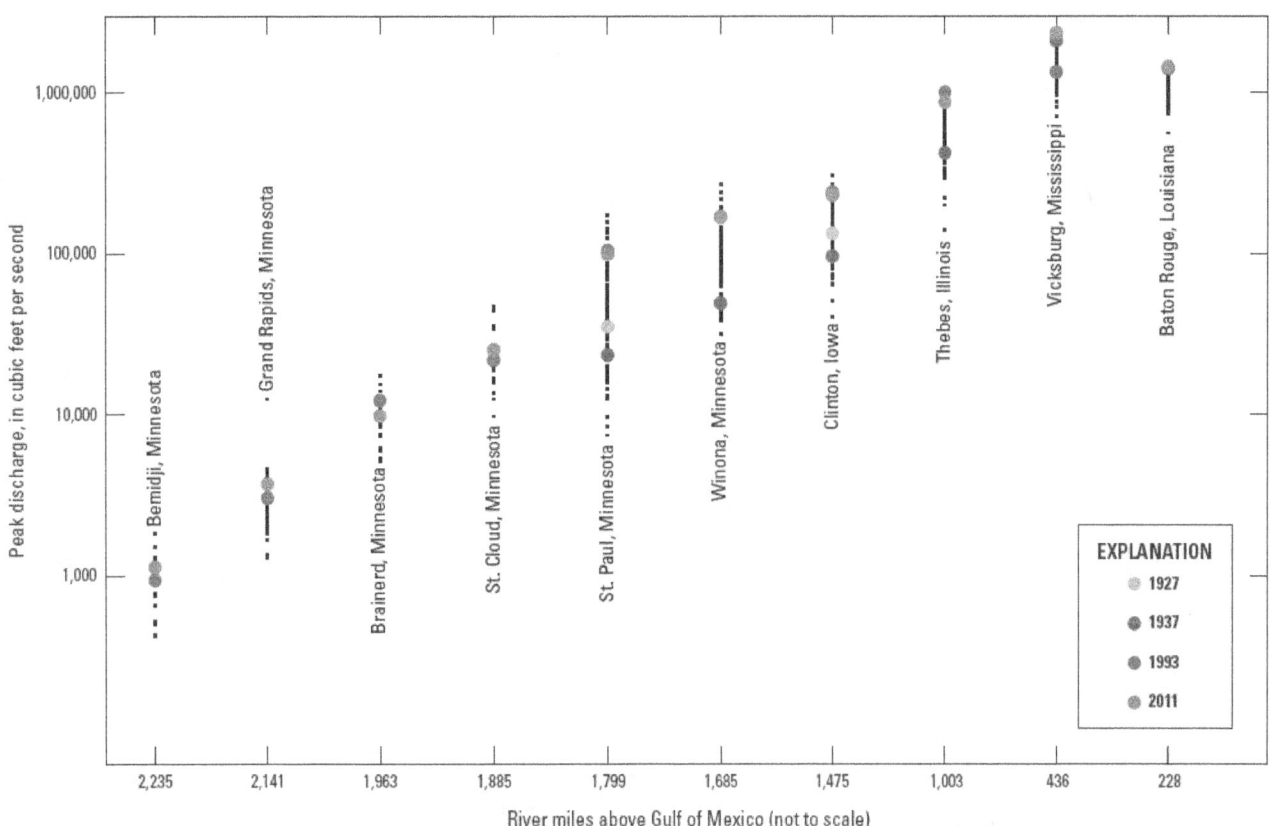

Figure 10.   2011 flood peaks on the Mississippi River in relation to other selected floods.

Morganza Floodway Control Structure in operation on May 22, 2011. Photograph by Robert Holmes, USGS.

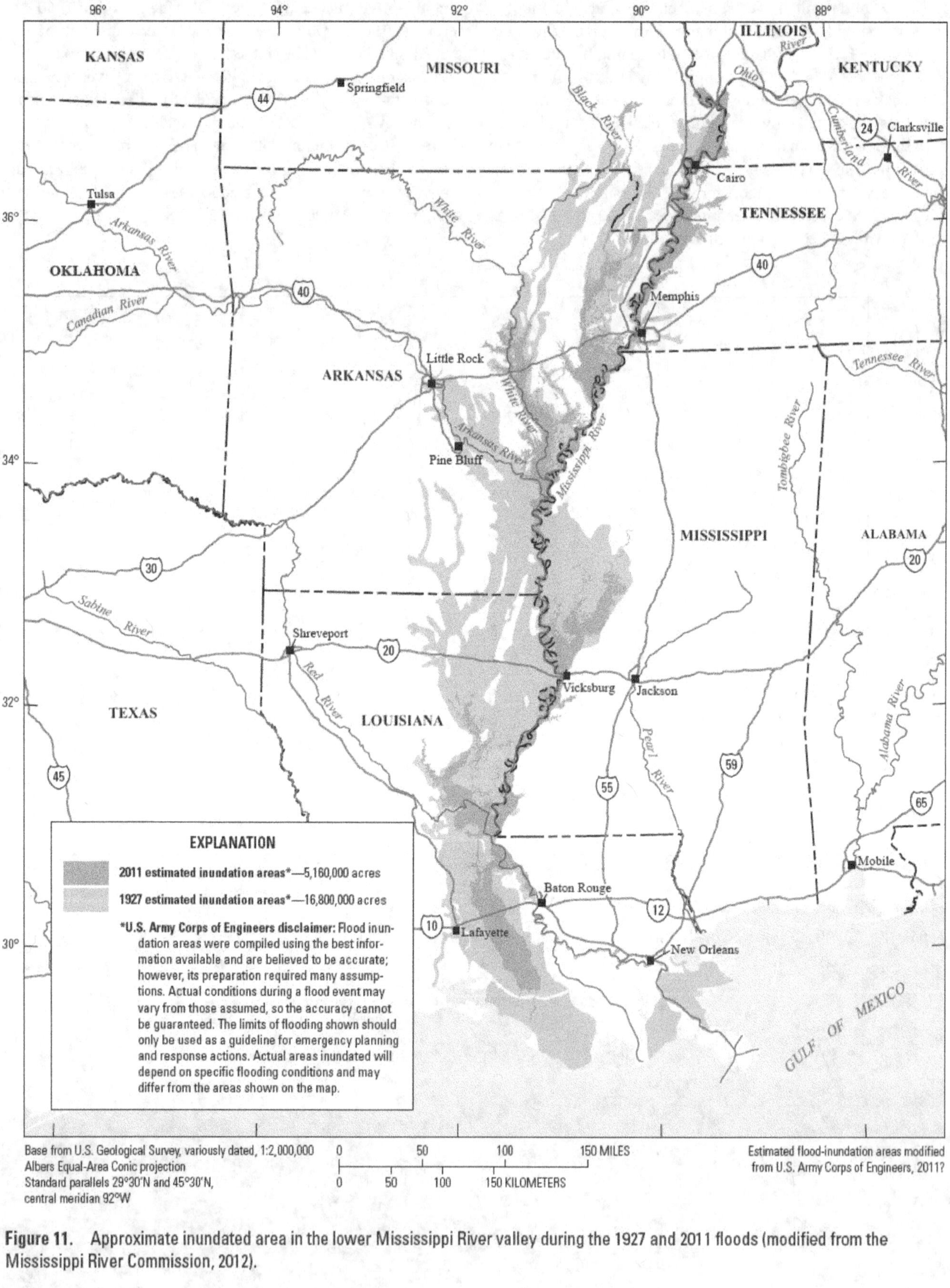
96°
94°
92°
90°
88°
36°
34°
32°
30°
KANSAS
MISSOURI
ILLINOIS
KENTUCKY
TENNESSEE
OKLAHOMA
ARKANSAS
MISSISSIPPI
ALABAMA
TEXAS
LOUISIANA
Springfield
Tulsa
Clarksville
Cairo
Memphis
Little Rock
Pine Bluff
Shreveport
Vicksburg
Jackson
Baton Rouge
Lafayette
New Orleans
Mobile
Illinois River
Ohio
Cumberland River
Black River
White River
Arkansas River
Canadian River
Mississippi River
Tennessee River
Tombigbee River
Sabine River
Red River
Pearl River
Alabama River
GULF OF MEXICO
44
24
40
30
20
55
59
65
45
10
12
EXPLANATION
2011 estimated inundation areas*—5,160,000 acres
1927 estimated inundation areas*—16,800,000 acres
*U.S. Army Corps of Engineers disclaimer: Flood inundation areas were compiled using the best information available and are believed to be accurate; however, its preparation required many assumptions. Actual conditions during a flood event may vary from those assumed, so the accuracy cannot be guaranteed. The limits of flooding shown should only be used as a guideline for emergency planning and response actions. Actual areas inundated will depend on specific flooding conditions and may differ from the areas shown on the map.
Base from U.S. Geological Survey, variously dated, 1:2,000,000
Albers Equal-Area Conic projection
Standard parallels 29°30'N and 45°30'N, central meridian 92°W
0 50 100 150 MILES
0 50 100 150 KILOMETERS
Estimated flood-inundation areas modified from U.S. Army Corps of Engineers, 2011?

Figure 11. Approximate inundated area in the lower Mississippi River valley during the 1927 and 2011 floods (modified from the Mississippi River Commission, 2012).

Source-area contributions to annual runoff volume
at Mississippi River at Vicksburg
(Water year is the 12-month period from October 1 through
September 30 and is designated by the year in which it ends)

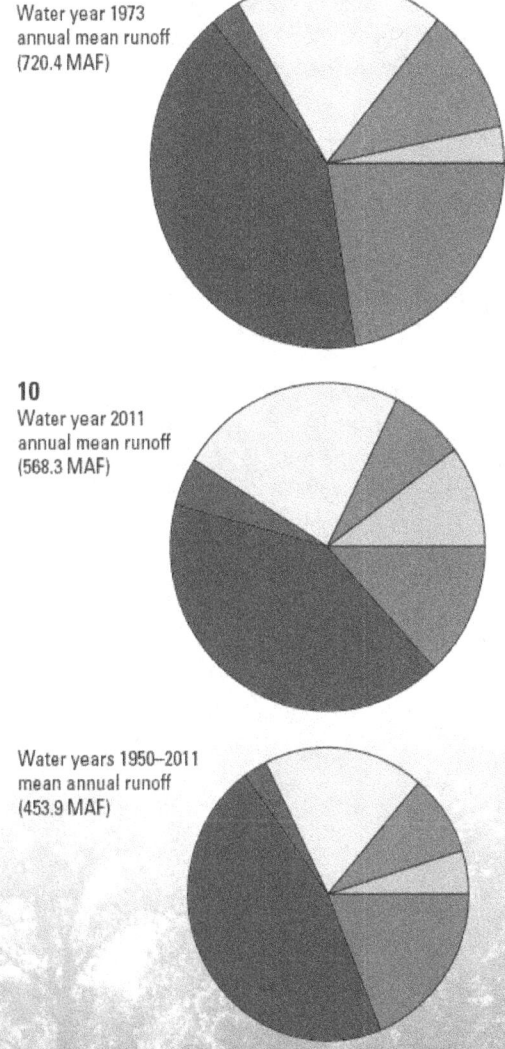

1
Water year 1973
annual mean runoff
(720.4 MAF)

10
Water year 2011
annual mean runoff
(568.3 MAF)

Water years 1950–2011
mean annual runoff
(453.9 MAF)

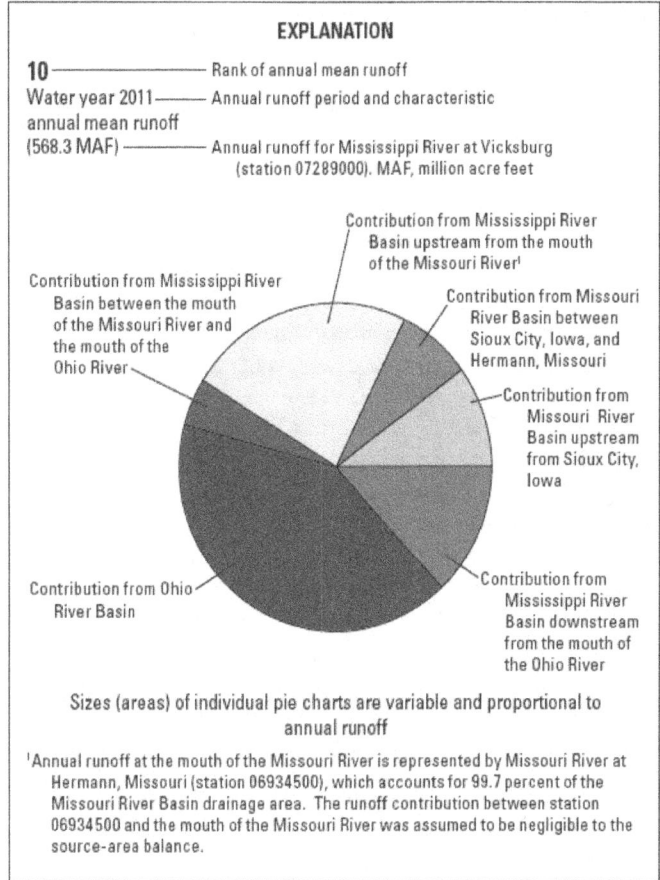

EXPLANATION

10 —————————— Rank of annual mean runoff

Water year 2011 ————— Annual runoff period and characteristic
annual mean runoff
(568.3 MAF) ————————— Annual runoff for Mississippi River at Vicksburg
(station 07289000). MAF, million acre feet

Contribution from Mississippi River
Basin upstream from the mouth
of the Missouri River[1]

Contribution from Mississippi River
Basin between the mouth
of the Missouri River and
the mouth of the
Ohio River

Contribution from Missouri
River Basin between
Sioux City, Iowa, and
Hermann, Missouri

Contribution from
Missouri River
Basin upstream
from Sioux City,
Iowa

Contribution from Ohio
River Basin

Contribution from
Mississippi River
Basin downstream
from the mouth of
the Ohio River

Sizes (areas) of individual pie charts are variable and proportional to
annual runoff

[1]Annual runoff at the mouth of the Missouri River is represented by Missouri River at
Hermann, Missouri (station 06934500), which accounts for 99.7 percent of the
Missouri River Basin drainage area. The runoff contribution between station
06934500 and the mouth of the Missouri River was assumed to be negligible to the
source-area balance.

Figure 12. Composition by selected upstream subbasins from the
annual runoff for the Mississippi River at Vicksburg, Mississippi (USGS
streamgage 07289000).

Electric powered water pumps are in danger of being flooded and put out of
commission by the rising Mississippi River in Vicksburg, Mississippi, May 6, 2011.
Photograph by Howard Greenblatt, Federal Emergency Management Agency (FEMA).

Summary

During 2011, flooding on numerous rivers in the Central United States, spanning from the Canadian border to the Gulf of Mexico and the Rocky Mountains to the Allegheny Mountains, resulted in 33 fatalities and approximately $4.2 billion in damages. The floods were the result of: (1) excess rainfall (in some locations rainfall was as much as 700- to 1,000- percent above normal), (2) melting of larger than normal snowpacks, or (3) a combination of excess rainfall and melting snow. The flooding began in late February 2011 in parts of the Mississippi River Basin and continued in parts of the Mississippi River Basin or Red/Souris River Basins until September 2011. Some locations received multiple flood pulses, such as the Souris River, which received two separate flood pulses, and the lower Mississippi River, which had three separate flood pulses pass through that reach.

Peak streamflow records were broken at 105 streamgages across the Souris/Red and Mississippi River Basins, with many previous peaks being longstanding records. For example, the record peak streamflow on the Souris River at Minot, N. Dak. broke the record set more than 100 years prior. The widespread major flooding in the upper Mississippi River, Missouri, and Ohio Basins during 2011 resulted in record peak streamflows in the lower Mississippi River; in some locations breaking the record peak streamflow magnitudes established during the 1927 flood. Annual runoff volume records were recorded at 47 of the 211 streamgages analyzed for annual runoff in the Souris/Red and Mississippi River Basins, with no annual runoff records occurring in the Ohio or lower Mississippi River Basins.

For the period of 1950 through 2011, the Ohio River provided almost one-half of the annual runoff at Vicksburg, Miss., the Missouri River contributed less than one-fourth, and the lower Mississippi River less than one-fourth. Those relative contribution patterns also occurred in 1973 and 2011; with the notable exception of the decrease in contribution of the lower Mississippi River tributaries and the increase in contribution from the upper Missouri River Basin in 2011 as compared to 1973 and the long-term average from 1950 to 2011.

U.S. Geological Survey boat nosed into shore loading research equipment before measurement downstream from the Old River Control Structure on May 22, 2011. Photograph by Robert Holmes, USGS.

References Cited

Camillo, C.A., 2012, Divine providence: Mississippi River Commission, 312 p.

Holmes, R.R., Jr., Koenig, T.A., and Karstensen, K.A., 2010, Flooding in the United States Midwest, 2008: U.S. Geological Survey Professional Paper 1775, 64 p. (Also available online at *http://pubs.usgs.gov/pp/1775/*.)

Mississippi River Commission, 1954, Annual highest and lowest stages of the Mississippi River and its outlets and tributaries to 1953, Vicksburg, Mississippi: 253 p.

Mississippi River Commission, 1955, Annual maximum minimum and mean discharges of the Mississippi River and its outlets and tributaries to 1953, Vicksburg, Mississippi, 140 p.

Mississippi River Commission, 2012, MR&T flood report, 45 p.

National Oceanic and Atmospheric Administration, 2012a, Service assessment Spring 2011 Middle and Lower Mississippi River Valley Floods: National Oceanic and Atmospheric Administration National Weather Service Report of March 2012, 54 p., accessed on May 30, 2012, at *http://www.nws.noaa.gov/om/assessments/pdfs/MisssissippiRiverFloods12.pdf*.

National Oceanic and Atmospheric Administration, 2012b, Service assessment of the Missouri/Souris River floods of May-August, 2011: National Oceanic and Atmospheric Administration National Weather Service Report of May 2012, 68 p., accessed on September 11, 2012, at *http://www.nws.noaa.gov/om/assessments/pdfs/Missouri_floods11.pdf*.

National Oceanic and Atmospheric Administration, 2011a, United States flood loss report—Water year 2011: National Oceanic and Atmospheric Administration, National Weather Service, accessed March 29, 2012, at *http://www.nws.noaa.gov/hic/summaries/WY2011.pdf*.

National Oceanic and Atmospheric Administration, 2011b, Another spring of major flooding likely in north central U.S.: National Oceanic and Atmospheric Administration, accessed November 3, 2011, at *http://www.noaanews.noaa.gov/stories2011/20110218_floodoutlook.html*.

National Weather Service, 2012, Advanced hydrologic prediction service precipitation: Archive of 1-day observed precipitation, National Weather Service, accessed on June 6, 2012, at *http://water.weather.gov/precip/*.

Parrett, Charles, Melcher, N.B., and James, Jr., R.W., 1993, Flood Discharges in the Upper Mississippi River Basin, 1993, U.S. Geological Survey Circular 1120–A, 14 p.

Southard, Rodney, 1995, Flood volumes in the Upper Mississippi River Basin, April 1 through September 30, 1993, U.S. Geological Survey Circular 1120–H, 32 p.

U.S. Army Corps of Engineers, 2012a, Summary of Engineering Data—Missouri River Main Stem System : Accessed June 6, 2012, at *http://www.nwd-mr.usace.army.mil/rcc/projdata/summaryengdat.pdf*.

U.S. Army Corps of Engineers, 2012b, Missouri River Mainstem Reservoir System—Summary of Actual 2011 Regulation Missouri River Basin: U.S. Army Corps of Engineers Northwestern Division, 90 p., accessed on September 11, 2012, at *http://www.nwd-mr.usace.army.mil/rcc/reports/pdfs/rcc2011summary.pdf*.

U.S. Army Corps of Engineers, 2012c, Post 2011 flood event analysis of the Missouri River mainstem flood control storage: U.S. Army Corps of Engineers Northwestern Division, 29 p., accessed on June 6, 2012, at *http://www.nwd-mr.usace.army.mil/rcc/reports/pdfs/Post2011FloodEventAnalysisofMainstemFloodControlStorage.pdf*.

U.S. Army Corps of Engineers, 2006, Missouri River Missouri River mainstem reservoir system master water control manual Missouri River Basin: 432 p., accessed on November 30, 2012, at *http://www.nwd-mr.usace.army.mil/rcc/reports/mmanual/MasterManual.pdf*.

U.S. Geological Survey, 2011, USGS water data for the nation, accessed June 10, 2012 at *http://waterdata.usgs.gov/nwis/*.

U.S. Geological Survey, 2012a, WaterWatch: Archive of streamflow maps (United States), November 15, 2010, U.S. Geological Survey, accessed on April 9, 2012, at *http://waterwatch.usgs.gov/?id=pamap*.

U.S. Geological Survey, 2012b, WaterWatch: Archive of streamflow maps (United States), March 1 to June 30, 2011, U.S. Geological Survey, accessed on June 6, 2012, at *http://waterwatch.usgs.gov/?id=pamap*.

Vining, K.C., Chase, K.J., and Loss, G.R., 2013, General weather conditions and precipitation contributing to the 2011 flooding in the Mississippi and Red River of the North Basins, December 2010 through July 2011: U.S. Geological Survey Professional Paper 1798–B, 22 p. (Also available online at *http://pubs.usgs.gov/pp/1798b/*.)

Watermolen, John, 2005, 1:2,000,000-Scale Hydrologic Unit Boundaries: National Atlas of the United States, Reston, VA. Available online at *http://nationalatlas.gov/mld/hucs00m.html*.

Winnipeg Free Press, 2011, Minot a wasteland after 'tsunami' hits, July 22, 2011, accessed on April 2, 2013, at *http://www.winnipegfreepress.com/local/minot-a-wasteland-after-tsunami-hits-126001723.html*.

U.S. Geological Survey hydrographers collecting streamflow data on the Mississippi River above the Morganza Floodway on May 22, 2011. Photograph by Robert Holmes, USGS.

Tables

Table 1. Peak streamflows at selected streamgages in the Central United States during the 2011 floods.

[mi², square miles; ft, feet; ft³/s, cubic feet per second; --, data not available; n/a, not applicable]

Map site number (fig. 4)	Station number	Station name	Contributing drainage area (mi²)	Previous maximum streamflow			Flood data			
				Date	Stage (ft)	Streamflow (ft³/s)	Rank[/]annual peaks in record	Date of peak streamflow	Floods of 2011 Peak stage (ft)	Peak streamflow (ft³/s)
		Red River of the North Basin								
1	05030500	Otter Tail River near Elizabeth, Minnesota	1,230	05/2009	9.66	[2]1,330	1/34	6/1/2011	[3]9.96	[2]1,360
2	05046000	Otter Tail River below Orwell Dam near Fergus Falls, Minnesota	1,740	05/2001	5.46	[2]2,040	3/81	5/2/2011	5.24	[2]2,010
3	05049000	Mustinka River above Wheaton, Minnesota	810	04/2001	[4]21.18	11,000	3/63	4/6/2011	94.61	7,730
4	05050000	Bois De Sioux River near White Rock, South Dakota	1,160	04/1997	16.90	[2]8,750	2/70	4/15/2011	[3]16.11	[2]6,770
5	05051500	Red River of the North at Wahpeton, North Dakota	4,010	04/1997	[5]19.25	[2]12,800	7/71	4/7/2011	15.69	[2]7,490
6	05051522	Red River of the North at Hickson, North Dakota	4,300	03/2009	39.04	[2]23,700	3/36	4/7/2011	37.15	[2]13,900
7	05051600	Wild Rice River near Rutland, North Dakota	296	04/1997	10.11	2,700	5/52	4/5/2011	[3,6]8.01	1,280
8	05052000	Wild Rice River near Mantador, North Dakota	1,160	03/2010	11.37	[2]4,730	2/35	4/11/2011	10.94	[2]4,060
9	05053000	Wild Rice River near Abercrombie, North Dakota	1,490	03/2009	27.78	[2]14,100	2/79	4/6/2011	25.99	[2]11,800
10	05054000	Red River of the North at Fargo, North Dakota	6,800	03/2009	40.84	[2]29,500	3/111	4/9/2011	38.81	[2]27,200
11	05054500	Sheyenne River above Harvey, North Dakota	424	04/2009	10.46	2,100	2/56	4/13/2011	10.52	2,010
12	05056000	Sheyenne River near Warwick, North Dakota	760	04/2009	8.43	4,930	1/62	4/11/2011	9.29	8,200
13	05056060	Mauvais Coulee Trib #3 near Cando, North Dakota	60.2	04/1969	9.35	2,300	2/42	4/14/2011	11.18	2,040
14	05056100	Mauvais Coulee near Cando, North Dakota	377	04/1997	11.68	3,000	1/54	4/15/2011	12.42	3,770
15	05056239	Starkweather Coulee near Webster, North Dakota	210	04/2009	8.58	978	3/32	4/16/2011	[3,6]9.61	885

Table 1. Peak streamflows at selected streamgages in the Central United States during the 2011 floods.—Continued

[mi², square miles; ft, feet; ft³/s, cubic feet per second; --, data not available; n/a, not applicable]

| Map site number (fig. 4) | Station number | Station name | Contributing drainage area (mi²) | Flood data | | | | | | |
| | | | | Previous maximum streamflow | | | | Floods of 2011 | | |
				Date	Stage (ft)	Streamflow (ft³/s)	Rank/annual peaks in record	Date of peak streamflow	Peak stage (ft)	Peak streamflow (ft³/s)
16	05057000	Sheyenne River near Cooperstown, North Dakota	1,270	04/1950	18.69	7,830	1/67	4/14/2011	19.51	8,460
17	05057200	Baldhill Creek near Dazey, North Dakota	351	04/1979	17.78	[7]9,000	4/56	4/10/2011	11.93	3,200
18	05058000	Sheyenne River below Baldhill Dam, North Dakota	1,910	04/2009	38.35	[2]6,200	1/63	4/13/2011	38.57	[2]7,060
19	05058500	Sheyenne River at Valley City, North Dakota	2,110	04/2009	[5]20.59	[2]7,940	2/73	4/18/2011	20.66	[2]7,270
20	05058700	Sheyenne River at Lisbon, North Dakota	2,490	04/2009	[5]22.86	[2]9,250	2/55	4/20/2011	21.70	[2]8,280
21	05059000	Sheyenne River near Kindred, North Dakota	3,020	04/1997	[5]21.38	[2]5,970	1/63	4/27/2011	[3]21.35	[2]6,290
22	05059500	Sheyenne River at West Fargo, North Dakota	3,090	04/1997	22.68	[2]4,810	1/86	4/29/2011	[3,6]22.80	[2]4,830
23	05059600	Maple River near Hope, North Dakota	17.4	03/2004	[5]6.98	1,000	1/47	8/1/2011	8.05	1,340
24	05059700	Maple River near Enderlin, North Dakota	796	06/1975	15.41	7,610	3/56	4/11/2011	13.31	6,830
25	05060400	Sheyenne River at Harwood, North Dakota	--	04/1997	92.02	[2,7]11,000	1/16	4/10/2011	91.82	[2]13,000
26	05060500	Rush River at Amenia, North Dakota	116	04/1979	[5]10.37	3,490	5/65	4/7/2011	11.00	1,970
29	05064500	Red River of the North at Halstad, Minnesota	21,800	04/1997	40.74	[2]71,500	3/72	4/12/2011	40.51	[2]60,700
30	05065500	Goose River near Portland, North Dakota	407	05/1950	[4]27.10	8,530	6/46	4/8/2011	25.15	3,220
31	05066500	Goose River at Hillsboro, North Dakota	1,093	04/1979	16.76	14,800	2/85	4/9/2011	15.50	10,000
32	05069000	Sand Hill River at Climax, Minnesota	420	04/1965	17.81	4,560	1/69	4/10/2011	[3,6]34.56	[7,8]4,800
33	05070000	Red River of the North near Thompson, North Dakota	24,010	04/2009	64.56	[2]61,300	1/13	4/13/2011	65.18	[2]72,000
34	05076000	Thief River near Thief River Falls, Minnesota	985	05/1950	17.38	5,610	3/100	4/6/2011	16.07	4,640

Table 1   27

Table 1. Peak streamflows at selected streamgages in the Central United States during the 2011 floods.—Continued

[mi², square miles; ft, feet; ft³/s, cubic feet per second; --, data not available; n/a, not applicable]

Map site number (fig. 4)	Station number	Station name	Contributing drainage area (mi²)	Previous maximum streamflow			Flood data / Floods of 2011			
				Date	Stage (ft)	Streamflow (ft³/s)	Rank/ annual peaks in record	Date of peak streamflow	Peak stage (ft)	Peak streamflow (ft³/s)
36	05082500	Red River of the North at Grand Forks, North Dakota	26,300	04/1997	[5]52.04	[2]137,000	2/130	4/14/2011	49.86	[2]87,500
37	05083500	Red River of the North at Oslo, Minnesota	27,400	04/1997	38.00	[2]120,000	2/49	4/14/2011	38.09	[2]81,400
41	05092000	Red River of the North at Drayton, North Dakota	34,800	04/1997	45.55	[2]124,000	5/74	4/19/2011	43.17	[2]83,000
43	05099600	Pembina River at Walhalla, North Dakota	3,350	04/1997	16.53	[9]23,100	4/65	4/18/2011	16.55	16,300
44	05100000	Pembina River at Neche, North Dakota	3,410	04/2009	21.61	16,900	2/104	4/19/2011	[3,6]21.78	15,300
		Souris River Basin								
46	05113600	Long Creek near Noonan, North Dakota	630	03/1976	17.61	6,310	1/52	6/21/2011	19.55	10,800
47	05114000	Souris River near Sherwood, North Dakota	3,040	04/1976	25.15	[2]14,800	1/82	6/23/2011	28.16	[2]29,700
48	05116000	Souris River near Foxholm, North Dakota	3,270	04/1976	17.17	[8]8,600	1/75	6/25/2011	22.44	[2]26,400
49	05116500	Des Lacs River at Foxholm, North Dakota	539	04/1979	21.23	[4]4,260	3/66	6/1/2011	20.57	[2]3,620
50	05117500	Souris River above Minot, North Dakota	3,900	04/1904	[4,7]21.90	[9]12,000	1/108	6/25/2011	24.37	[2]26,900
51	05120000	Souris River near Verendrye, North Dakota	4,400	04/2009	17.92	[2]10,900	1/75	6/26/2011	18.53	[2]26,900
52	05120500	Wintering River near Karlsruhe, North Dakota	285	04/1949	[6]12.00	[2]3,000	6/75	4/12/2011	[3,6]8.87	[2]1,360
53	05122000	Souris River near Bantry, North Dakota	4,700	04/1976	14.59	[2]9,330	1/75	6/28/2011	16.90	[2]30,000
54	05123400	Willow Creek near Willow City, North Dakota	730	04/1969	16.76	5,900	4/55	4/12/2011	15.24	2,900
55	05123510	Deep River near Upham, North Dakota	370	04/1969	18.18	6,760	2/49	4/11/2011	17.62	5,110
56	05124000	Souris River near Westhope, North Dakota	6,600	04/1976	19.16	[2]12,600	1/82	7/5/2011	[3]22.95	[2]30,400

Table 1   29

Table 1. Peak streamflows at selected streamgages in the Central United States during the 2011 floods.—Continued

[mi², square miles; ft, feet; ft³/s, cubic feet per second; --, data not available; n/a, not applicable]

Map site number (fig. 4)	Station number	Station name	Contributing drainage area (mi²)	Previous maximum streamflow			Flood data			
							Floods of 2011			
				Date	Stage (ft)	Streamflow (ft³/s)	Rank[1]/annual peaks in record	Date of peak streamflow	Peak stage (ft)	Peak streamflow (ft³/s)
		Upper Mississippi River Basin (upstream of the mouth of the Ohio River), excluding the Missouri River Basin								
61	05278930	Buffalo Creek near Glencoe, Minnesota	373	09/1991	11.78	[10]4,300	4/27	3/25/2011	[3,6]19.59	3,490
62	05280000	Crow River at Rockford, Minnesota	2,640	04/1965	19.27	22,400	9/90	4/10/2011	13.82	11,700
64	05287890	Elm Creek near Champlin, Minnesota	86.0	04/2001	10.02	875	3/33	3/24/2011	9.81	803
66	05288705	Shingle Creek at Queen Ave In Minneapolis, Minnesota	28.2	09/2005	13.26	[11]291	1/15	7/16/2011	[6]13.93	[11]301
67	05292000	Minnesota River at Ortonville, Minnesota	1,160	03/2010	12.84	[2]5,680	5/74	4/9/2011	10.28	[2]3,840
68	05293371	Pomme De Terre River below Elbow Lake, Minnesota	340	03/2009	6.81	744	1/26	7/15/2011	7.36	910
69	05294000	Pomme De Terre River at Appleton, Minnesota	905	04/1997	18.13	[12]8,890	7/79	4/6/2011	11.00	3,170
71	05301000	Minnesota River near Lac Qui Parle, Minnesota	4,050	04/1997	--	[2,7,9]43,000	5/66	4/6/2011	38.30	[2]19,700
72	05311000	Minnesota River at Montevideo, Minnesota	6,180	04/1997	23.90	[2]47,500	6/102	4/7/2011	19.76	[2]23,700
73	05313500	Yellow Medicine River near Granite Falls, Minnesota	664	04/1969	14.90	17,200	8/80	3/25/2011	9.77	6,620
74	05316500	Redwood River near Redwood Falls, Minnesota	629	06/1957	15.92	19,700	6/86	3/25/2011	[3,6]15.51	[7,8]7,370
75	05316950	Cottonwood River near Springfield, Minnesota	777	04/1969	31.55	[9]18,300	4/40	3/23/2011	30.06	9,480
76	05317000	Cottonwood River near New Ulm, Minnesota	1,300	04/1969	19.15	28,700	6/85	3/24/2011	17.15	15,100
77	05319500	Watonwan River near Garden City, Minnesota	851	04/1965	18.89	[9]19,000	6/44	3/24/2011	13.64	9,730
78	05320000	Blue Earth River near Rapidan, Minnesota	2,410	04/1965	21.36	43,100	7/99	3/22/2011	12.70	[2]18,600
79	05320270	Little Cobb River near Beauford, Minnesota	130	09/2010	15.31	5,120	2/15	3/20/2011	13.62	3,380
80	05320480	Maple River near Rapidan, Minnesota	338	09/2010	18.30	12,800	4/40	3/20/2011	13.09	4,660

Table 1. Peak streamflows at selected streamgages in the Central United States during the 2011 floods.—Continued

[mi², square miles; ft, feet; ft³/s, cubic feet per second; --, data not available; n/a, not applicable]

Map site number (fig. 4)	Station number	Station name	Contributing drainage area (mi²)	Previous maximum streamflow			Flood data — Floods of 2011			
				Date	Stage (ft)	Streamflow (ft³/s)	Rank[1]/annual peaks in record	Date of peak streamflow	Peak stage (ft)	Peak streamflow (ft³/s)
81	05320500	Le Sueur River near Rapidan, Minnesota	1,110	09/2010	21.35	30,500	4/69	3/21/2011	12.45	14,200
82	05325000	Minnesota River at Mankato, Minnesota	14,900	04/1965	29.09	94,100	8/109	3/26/2011	25.51	64,900
83	05330000	Minnesota River near Jordan, Minnesota	16,200	04/1965	[4,5]33.89	117,000	7/77	3/28/2011	31.81	72,300
84	05331000	Mississippi River at Saint Paul, Minnesota	36,800	04/1965	26.01	[2]171,000	7/119	3/29/2011	[3]19.04	[2]103,000
86	05344500	Mississippi River at Prescott, Wisconsin	44,800	04/1965	43.11	228,000	8/83	4/12/2011	[3]36.76	125,000
87	05348550	Cannon River below Sabre Lake near Kilkenny, Minnesota	87.9	04/2001	13.83	563	3/26	7/16/2011	13.91	497
90	05378500	Mississippi River at Winona, Minnesota	59,200	04/1965	20.77	268,000	7/83	4/15/2011	16.58	170,000
92	05389500	Mississippi River at McGregor, Iowa	67,500	04/1965	25.38	[2,8]276,000	10/74	4/17/2011	[3]21.38	[2]182,000
93	05394500	Prairie River Near Merrill, Wisconsin	184	08/1941	9.45	5,800	7/90	4/12/2011	7.62	2,550
94	05398000	Wisconsin River at Rothschild, Wisconsin	4,020	09/1941	22.30	[2,9]75,000	6/68	4/11/2011	28.17	[2]48,000
97	05414350	Little Maquoketa River near Graf, Iowa	39.6	06/2008	16.47	8,370	1/61	7/28/2011	17.48	9,420
98	05414400	Middle Fork Little Maquoketa River near Rickardsville, Iowa	30.2	08/1972	27.70	23,000	8/58	7/28/2011	19.81	7,510
99	05414450	North Fork Little Maquoketa River near Rickardsville, Iowa	21.6	06/2008	12.58	8,040	3/61	7/28/2011	14.88	6,690
100	05414605	Bloody Run Tributary near Sherrill, Iowa	0.6	06/2008	22.71	1,110	3/21	7/28/2011	18.63	624
101	05418400	North Fork Maquoketa River near Fulton, Iowa	505	07/2010	22.44	25,000	4/13	7/29/2011	19.53	17,100
102	05420500	Mississippi River at Clinton, Iowa	85,600	04/1965	24.65	[2,8]307,000	10/138	4/20/2011	[3]21.93	[2]229,000
107	05451080	South Fork Iowa River near Blairsburg, Iowa	12.0	06/2008	12.50	762	3/6	2/16/2011	11.14	564

Table 1. Peak streamflows at selected streamgages in the Central United States during the 2011 floods.—Continued

[mi², square miles; ft, feet; ft³/s, cubic feet per second; --, data not available; n/a, not applicable]

Table 1   31

Map site number (fig. 4)	Station number	Station name	Contributing drainage area (mi²)	Flood data						
				Previous maximum streamflow			Floods of 2011			
				Date	Stage (ft)	Streamflow (ft³/s)	Rank/ annual peaks in record	Date of peak streamflow	Peak stage (ft)	Peak streamflow (ft³/s)
111	05465150	North Fork Long Creek at Ainsworth, Iowa	30.2	06/1990	90.66	[7]5,800	7/48	6/15/2011	91.88	3,330
113	05469350	Haight Creek at Kingston, Iowa	2.7	05/2010	20.17	3,170	2/22	6/15/2011	19.60	2,940
114	05474500	Mississippi River at Keokuk, Iowa	119,000	07/1993	27.58	[2,13]446,000	11/134	4/25/2011	18.98	[2,8,13]276,000
115	05474900	Elk Creek On CSAH 1 near Brewster, Minnesota	61.0	05/2001	25.59	4,360	2/11	7/12/2011	25.29	3,680
116	05476000	Des Moines River at Jackson, Minnesota	1,250	04/1969	19.45	15,700	7/86	3/26/2011	15.69	6,860
121	05486490	Middle River near Indianola, Iowa	489	06/1947	[4]26.40	34,000	4/72	6/10/2011	24.08	15,100
122	05488110	Des Moines River near Pella, Iowa	12,330	07/1993	109.71	[2]105,000	5/19	7/20/2011	96.39	[2]31,000
123	05488500	Des Moines River near Tracy, Iowa	12,479	06/1947	26.50	155,000	34/93	6/28/2011	13.27	[2]33,500
124	05489500	Des Moines River at Ottumwa, Iowa	13,374	05/1903	19.40	[7]140,000	16/96	6/15/2011	14.90	[2]49,400
125	05490500	Des Moines River at Keosauqua, Iowa	14,038	06/1903	27.85	146,000	13/104	6/15/2011	[2]25.81	[2]69,900
126	05495000	Fox River at Wayland, Missouri	400	04/1973	21.71	26,400	2/90	6/15/2011	23.07	26,200
127	05496000	Wyaconda River above Canton, Missouri	393	06/1933	[7]30.00	17,700	6/86	6/16/2011	28.25	13,700
139	05587450	Mississippi River at Grafton, Illinois	171,300	08/1993	38.17	[2]598,000	7/25	5/1/2011	25.93	[2]362,000
140	05592100	Kaskaskia River at Cowden, Illinois	1,330	05/2002	20.36	[2]25,300	3/41	4/26/2011	18.88	[2]17,000
142	05592575	Hickory Creek near Brownstown, Illinois	44.2	11/1993	16.43	6,250	1/23	4/26/2011	16.88	6,880
145	055994490	Big Muddy River at Route 127 at Murphysboro, Illinois	2,159	03/2008	37.24	[2]31,500	5/84	5/2/2011	[3]40.47	242,400
146	07010000	Mississippi River at St. Louis, Missouri	697,000	08/1993	49.58	[2]1,070,000	45/151	4/30/2011	34.93	[2]615,000
148	07020500	Mississippi River at Chester, Illinois	708,600	04/1927	34.40	[2,8]1,060,000	18/87	5/2/2011	39.74	[2]703,000
149	07022000	Mississippi River at Thebes, Illinois	713,200	07/1844	--	[2,9]1,075,000	5/80	5/2/2011	[2]45.52	[2]876,000
		Missouri River Basin								
150	06012500	Red Rock River below Lima Reservoir near Monida, Montana	570	05/1933	5.40	[2]2,500	10/87	6/13/2011	4.03	[2]860
151	06015430	Clark Canyon near Dillon, Montana	18.0	05/1984	7.10	415	2/39	6/8/2011	6.10	315

Table 1. Peak streamflows at selected streamgages in the Central United States during the 2011 floods.—Continued

[mi², square miles; ft, feet; ft³/s, cubic feet per second; --, data not available; n/a, not applicable]

Map site number (fig. 4)	Station number	Station name	Contributing drainage area (mi²)	Previous maximum streamflow			Flood data	Floods of 2011		
				Date	Stage (ft)	Streamflow (ft³/s)	Rank/annual peaks in record	Date of peak streamflow	Peak stage (ft)	Peak streamflow (ft³/s)
152	06019500	Ruby River above reservoir near Alder, Montana	534	05/1984	6.24	3,810	5/73	6/8/2011	6.07	1,780
153	06020600	Ruby River below reservoir near Alder, Montana	596	05/1984	8.52	[2]3,010	3/49	6/9/2011	6.31	[2]1,720
154	06023000	Ruby River near Twin Bridges, Montana	965	06/1947	6.89	1,500	1/27	7/1/2011	5.81	1,630
155	06023100	Beaverhead River at Twin Bridges, Montana	4,779	06/2010	5.52	2,830	2/3	7/1/2011	5.50	2,800
156	06024540	Big Hole River below Mudd Creek near Wisdom, Montana	1,267	06/2010	6.47	5,580	1/14	6/10/2011	6.68	6,660
157	06024580	Big Hole River near Wise River, Montana	1,611	06/2010	6.85	8,100	1/5	6/11/2011	7.14	9,130
158	06026210	Big Hole River near Glen, Montana	2,655	06/2010	7.16	10,400	1/14	6/10/2011	7.63	11,900
159	06031950	Cataract Creek near Basin, Montana	30.6	05/1981	6.88	3,150	3/39	6/7/2011	3.38	820
160	06033000	Boulder River near Boulder, Montana	381	05/1981	12.30	[9]7,000	2/72	6/7/2011	10.15	3,520
161	06036650	Jefferson River near Three Forks, Montana	9,532	06/1995	9.00	17,000	1/33	6/12/2011	9.38	17,400
162	06036905	Firehole River near West Yellowstone, Montana	282	05/1996	6.10	2,050	2/22	6/8/2011	5.40	1,570
163	06037500	Madison River near West Yellowstone, Montana	420	05/1996	3.78	2,820	3/85	6/8/2011	3.51	2,520
164	06040800	Madison River above powerplant near McAllister, Montana	2,186	06/2010	9.53	[2]4,220	1/10	6/24/2011	10.80	[2]5,940
166	06043500	Gallatin River near Gallatin Gateway, Montana	825	06/1997	6.71	9,160	3/83	6/30/2011	6.51	8,410
167	06052500	Gallatin River at Logan, Montana	1,795	06/1899	--	9,840	7/92	6/30/2011	[3,6]9.57	7,980
168	06054500	Missouri River at Toston, Montana	14,669	06/1997	12.22	34,000	4/79	6/15/2011	11.53	29,500
169	06056300	Cabin Creek near Townsend, Montana	11.8	06/1960	2.00	70	1/52	5/9/2011	3.49	120
170	06061500	Prickly Pear Creek near Clancy, Montana	192	05/1981	8.82	2,300	3/71	6/7/2011	5.37	1,030

Table 1   33

Table 1. Peak streamflows at selected streamgages in the Central United States during the 2011 floods.—Continued

[mi², square miles; ft, feet; ft³/s, cubic feet per second; --, data not available; n/a, not applicable]

Map site number (fig. 4)	Station number	Station name	Contributing drainage area (mi²)	Previous maximum streamflow			Flood data Rank/annual peaks in record	Floods of 2011		
				Date	Stage (ft)	Streamflow (ft³/s)		Date of peak streamflow	Peak stage (ft)	Peak streamflow (ft³/s)
171	06062500	Tennile Creek near Rimini, Montana	30.9	05/1981	6.20	3,290	4/95	6/7/2011	4.31	742
172	06071300	Little Prickly Pear Creek at Wolf Creek, Montana	381	05/1975	7.45	[9]4,500	3/26	6/9/2011	7.84	2,460
173	06076690	Smith River near Fort Logan, Montana	846	05/1981	7.80	4,600	3/23	6/10/2011	6.70	2,270
174	06077200	Smith River below Eagle Creek near Fort Logan, Montana	1,088	06/1997	[5]7.00	3,900	1/15	6/9/2011	7.65	4,030
175	06077500	Smith River near Eden, Montana	1,594	06/1953	10.46	12,300	3/27	6/10/2011	8.77	5,710
176	06078200	Missouri River near Ulm, Montana	20,941	06/1953	17.00	[2,9,14]35,000	3/56	6/11/2011	15.48	[2]28,800
177	06089000	Sun River near Vaughn, Montana	1,849	06/1964	23.40	53,500	4/78	6/10/2011	8.29	14,800
178	06090300	Missouri River near Great Falls, Montana	23,292	06/1964	--	[2,8]72,000	5/60	6/11/2011	8.10	[2]38,800
179	06090650	Lake Creek near Power, Montana	83.8	03/1993	7.30	[8]300	2/22	6/7/2011	3.53	223
180	06090800	Missouri River at Fort Benton, Montana	24,749	06/1908	[7]18.50	[7]140,000	10/120	6/10/2011	[3,6]11.79	[2]52,700
181	06091700	Two Medicine River below South Fork, Near Browning, Montana	250	05/1991	7.78	11,700	4/35	6/7/2011	7.94	6,450
182	06099500	Marias River near Shelby, Montana	3,242	06/1964	23.64	[12]241,000	10/105	6/10/2011	12.11	18,800
184	06108800	Teton River at Loma, Montana	2,010	06/2002	5.87	2,000	1/14	6/12/2011	8.52	3,910
185	06109500	Missouri River at Virgelle, Montana	34,379	06/1953	--	[2,7]122,000	6/77	6/12/2011	14.07	[2]53,700
186	06112800	Bull Creek Tributary near Hilger, Montana	1.0	06/1991	5.69	415	2/38	5/21/2011	5.16	114
187	06114550	Wolf Creek Tributary near Coffee Creek, Montana	1.7	07/1978	5.55	780	4/38	6/9/2011	6.05	190
188	06114700	Judith River near mouth, Near Winifred, Montana	2,731	03/2003	[5]9.06	7,600	1/11	5/26/2011	10.46	15,300
189	06115200	Missouri River near Landusky, Montana	40,987	06/1953	--	[2]137,000	6/78	6/11/2011	32.35	[2]74,800
190	06120500	Musselshell River at Harlowton, Montana	1,125	06/1975	10.01	7,270	2/103	5/25/2011	10.25	5,520

Table 1. Peak streamflows at selected streamgages in the Central United States during the 2011 floods.—Continued

[mi², square miles; ft, feet; ft³/s, cubic feet per second; --, data not available; n/a, not applicable]

Map site number (fig. 4)	Station number	Station name	Contributing drainage area (mi²)	Previous maximum streamflow			Flood data	Floods of 2011		
				Date	Stage (ft)	Streamflow (ft³/s)	Rank[1]/ annual peaks in record	Date of peak streamflow	Peak stage (ft)	Peak streamflow (ft³/s)
191	06123030	Musselshell River above Mud Creek near Shawmut, Montana	1,513	06/2010	5.76	1,290	1/14	5/26/2011	9.27	8,900
192	06126050	Musselshell River near Lavina, Montana	2,970	06/1997	11.13	[2]6,220	1/20	5/25/2011	13.95	[2]14,500
193	06126500	Musselshell River near Roundup, Montana	4,023	06/1967	12.45	[2]9,610	1/65	5/26/2011	14.78	[2]15,000
194	06127500	Musselshell River at Musselshell, Montana	4,568	06/1967	11.57	[2]9,850	1/66	5/27/2011	13.23	[2]16,200
195	06127520	Home Creek near Sumatra, Montana	2.0	03/1994	5.11	278	2/39	5/10/2011	5.10	164
196	06127570	Butts Coulee near Melstone, Montana	6.7	07/1993	20.18	705	4/49	5/10/2011	14.53	402
197	06127585	Little Wall Creek Tributary near Flatwillow, Montana	9.8	07/2009	6.78	45	1/38	6/7/2011	8.54	326
198	06129000	Box Elder Creek near Winnett, Montana	684	06/1962	15.34	9,910	2/22	5/22/2011	--	[9]9,450
199	06130500	Musselshell River at Mosby, Montana	7,846	06/1944	--	18,000	1/80	5/23/2011	15.98	25,100
200	06130915	Russian Coulee near Jordan, Montana	3.5	08/1993	7.45	840	3/38	5/21/2011	6.05	276
201	06132000	Missouri River below Fort Peck Dam, Montana	57,556	08/1946	--	[2]51,000	1/78	6/15/2011	[3]15.53	[2,8]65,900
202	06142400	Clear Creek near Chinook, Montana	135	09/1986	8.21	571	2/28	6/4/2011	8.44	571
203	06144450	Middle Creek above Lodge Creek near Govenlock, Saskatchewan	276	09/1986	13.84	738	3/25	4/27/2011	9.89	494
204	06154100	Milk River near Harlem, Montana	9,822	1952	--	[7,8,9,14]19,000	6/41	6/11/2011	23.46	[2]6,380
205	06155030	Milk River near Dodson, Montana	11,192	09/1986	29.79	13,200	2/29	5/23/2011	26.25	8,550
206	06164510	Milk River at Juneberg Bridge near Saco, Montana	17,670	04/1978	24.20	[2]12,400	5/34	4/14/2011	22.07	[2]10,300
207	06166000	Beaver Creek below Guston Coulee near Saco, Montana	1,208	09/1986	14.68	23,500	2/29	6/13/2011	[3,6]12.93	3,350
208	06167500	Beaver Creek near Hinsdale, Montana	1,785	06/2007	16.00	2,050	1/7	6/9/2011	19.44	8,210
209	06172310	Milk River at Tampico, Montana	21,078	03/1997	--	[7,8]11,000	1/28	4/15/2011	28.03	19,700
210	06174500	Milk River at Nashua, Montana	22,332	04/1952	31.38	[2]45,300	2/72	6/9/2011	29.52	[2]26,500

Table 1   35

Table 1. Peak streamflows at selected streamgages in the Central United States during the 2011 floods.—Continued

[mi², square miles; ft, feet; ft³/s, cubic feet per second; --, data not available; n/a, not applicable]

Map site number (fig. 4)	Station number	Station name	Contributing drainage area (mi²)	Previous maximum streamflow Date	Stage (ft)	Streamflow (ft³/s)	Flood data Rank[1]/ annual peaks in record	Floods of 2011 Date of peak streamflow	Peak stage (ft)	Peak streamflow (ft³/s)
211	06177000	Missouri River near Wolf Point, Montana	82,290	03/1939	[6]14.40	[2,]66,800	1/83	6/14/2011	14.77	[2]93,200
212	06178500	East Poplar River at international boundary, Montana	541	04/1975	12.01	[2]4,020	12/78	4/12/2011	11.41	1,830
213	06185500	Missouri River near Culbertson, Montana	91,557	03/1943	[6]15.12	[2]78,200	1/63	6/16/2011	17.50	[2]104,000
214	06186500	Yellowstone River at Yellowstone Lake Outlet, Wyoming	991	06/1997	8.90	9,950	2/86	7/11/2011	8.74	9,560
215	06187915	Soda Butte Creek at Park Boundary at Silver Gate, Montana	31.2	06/2010	3.83	1,250	2/13	6/30/2011	3.85	1,230
216	06188000	Lamar River near Tower Ranger Station, Wyoming	660	06/1996	12.15	19,500	4/72	6/24/2011	10.75	15,500
217	06191500	Yellowstone River at Corwin Springs, Montana	2,619	06/1996	10.92	32,200	5/105	6/30/2011	10.36	30,300
218	06192500	Yellowstone River near Livingston, Montana	3,551	06/1997	10.72	38,000	1/87	6/30/2011	10.15	40,600
219	06195600	Shields River near Livingston, Montana	852	06/1979	6.80	5,600	2/33	5/25/2011	6.36	4,360
220	06200000	Boulder River at Big Timber, Montana	523	06/1997	9.00	9,940	4/64	6/30/2011	8.04	9,370
221	06205000	Stillwater River near Absarokee, Montana	935	06/1967	7.17	12,000	6/81	6/30/2011	6.86	9,950
222	06207500	Clarks Fork Yellowstone River near Belfry, Montana	1,154	06/1981	9.97	14,800	3/90	7/5/2011	8.68	12,500
223	06208500	Clarks Fork Yellowstone River at Edgar, Montana	2,022	06/1997	9.30	11,100	5/72	7/6/2011	9.27	10,700
224	06209500	Rock Creek near Red Lodge, Montana	105	06/1957	4.78	3,110	4/63	6/29/2011	7.78	2,040
225	06211000	Red Lodge Creek above Cooney Reservoir near Boyd, Montana	143	05/2005	7.35	3,720	1/75	5/25/2011	7.74	4,700
226	06211500	Willow Creek near Boyd, Montana	53.3	05/2005	8.59	2,100	1/75	5/25/2011	8.60	2,110
227	06214500	Yellowstone River at Billings, Montana	11,408	06/1997	15.00	82,000	3/86	7/2/2011	14.37	70,600

Table 1. Peak streamflows at selected streamgages in the Central United States during the 2011 floods.—Continued

[mi², square miles; ft, feet; ft³/s, cubic feet per second; --, data not available; n/a, not applicable]

Map site number (fig. 4)	Station number	Station name	Contributing drainage area (mi²)	Previous maximum streamflow			Flood data — Floods of 2011			
				Date	Stage (ft)	Streamflow (ft³/s)	Rank/annual peaks in record	Date of peak streamflow	Peak stage (ft)	Peak streamflow (ft³/s)
228	06217300	Twelvemile Creek near Shepherd, Montana	9.1	06/2001	10.25	1,230	2/39	5/24/2011	4.23	395
229	06218500	Wind River near Dubois, Wyoming	232	06/1972	[5]5.48	[2]1,940	1/57	7/1/2011	5.65	[2]2,040
230	06224000	Bull Lake Creek above Bull Lake, Wyoming	187	06/1981	7.98	4,470	2/58	7/1/2011	7.22	4,310
231	06225500	Wind River near Crowheart, Wyoming	1,891	06/1991	11.04	[2]14,300	1/67	6/30/2011	10.87	[2]14,700
232	06227600	Wind River near Kinnear, Wyoming	2,194	06/1991	8.03	[2]13,900	1/27	7/2/2011	[7,9]9.92	[2,7]16,600
233	06228000	Wind River at Riverton, Wyoming	2,309	06/1935	[8]8.15	[2]13,300	5/103	7/2/2011	11.80	[2]11,200
234	06236100	Wind River above Boysen Reservoir near Shoshoni, Wyoming	4,390	06/2010	9.19	[2]19,200	2/21	7/2/2011	9.07	[2]18,700
235	06278300	Shell Creek above Shell Creek Reservoir, Wyoming	23.1	06/1963	[7]7.84	1,870	2/55	6/29/2011	7.58	1,480
236	06278500	Shell Creek near Shell, Wyoming	145	06/1945	7.49	[2]3,020	1/70	6/29/2011	7.32	[2]4,850
237	06280300	South Fork Shoshone River near Valley, Wyoming	297	06/1981	9.24	[2]10,000	2/54	6/29/2011	7.93	[2]7,560
238	06281000	South Fork Shoshone River above Buffalo Bill Reservoir, Wyoming	585	06/1981	9.41	[2]9,960	4/48	6/30/2011	9.28	[2]7,530
240	06289820	East Pass Creek near Dayton, Wyoming	21.7	06/2007	[4]7.64	[2]755	2/29	5/21/2011	[3]9.05	[2]732
241	06291000	Owl Creek near Lodge Grass, Montana	163	06/1944	14.18	1,020	1/20	5/25/2011	--	[9]4,810
242	06293300	Long Otter Creek near Lodge Grass, Montana	11.7	05/2008	9.18	360	3/39	5/22/2011	5.96	192
243	06294000	Little Bighorn River near Hardin, Montana	1,294	05/1978	11.20	22,600	2/59	5/23/2011	12.32	17,300
244	06294400	Andresen Coulee near Custer, Montana	2.4	06/1991	4.40	255	3/49	3/10/2011	3.32	155
245	06294500	Bighorn River above Tullock Creek near Bighorn, Montana	22,414	06/1991	[5]7.17	[2]16,100	1/47	5/23/2011	10.86	[2]33,200
246	06294930	Sarpy Creek Tributary near Colstrip, Montana	4.4	03/1978	4.84	590	5/40	5/21/2011	6.29	120
247	06294985	East Fork Armells Creek Tributary near Colstrip, Montana	1.9	07/1993	3.71	357	2/39	5/21/2011	3.44	291

Table 1   37

Table 1. Peak streamflows at selected streamgages in the Central United States during the 2011 floods.—Continued

[mi², square miles; ft, feet; ft³/s, cubic feet per second; --, data not available; n/a, not applicable]

Map site number (fig. 4)	Station number	Station name	Contributing drainage area (mi²)	Previous maximum streamflow			Flood data — Floods of 2011			
				Date	Stage (ft)	Streamflow (ft³/s)	Rank/ annual peaks in record	Date of peak streamflow	Peak stage (ft)	Peak streamflow (ft³/s)
248	06295000	Yellowstone River at Forsyth, Montana	39,455	05/1978	14.53	109,800	2/37	5/24/2011	12.24	78,800
249	06295113	Rosebud Creek at Reservation Boundary near Kirby, Montana	123	03/1996	[5]6.30	219	1/32	5/22/2011	10.71	1,720
250	06307616	Tongue River at Birney Day School Bridge near Birney, Montana	2,621	06/2007	7.06	[2]5,340	3/32	6/12/2011	7.30	[2]4,430
251	06307740	Otter Creek at Ashland, Montana	707	03/1978	[6]8.65	425	3/29	5/25/2011	5.51	347
252	06307990	Tongue River above T&Y Diversion Dam near Miles City, Montana	4,508	06/2007	10.40	[2]7,510	2/7	5/22/2011	9.50	[2]6,280
253	06308340	La Grange Creek near Volborg, Montana	3.7	07/1993	9.65	550	5/38	5/23/2011	8.50	208
254	06308400	Pumpkin Creek near Miles City, Montana	697	05/1975	12.27	2,890	1/20	5/20/2011	14.41	7,900
255	06308500	Tongue River at Miles City, Montana	5,397	06/1962	11.33	[2]13,300	1/70	5/21/2011	13.99	[2]15,300
256	06309000	Yellowstone River at Miles City, Montana	48,253	05/1978	16.50	[2]102,000	3/84	5/24/2011	14.74	[2]85,400
257	06311000	North Fork Powder River near Hazelton, Wyoming	24.5	06/1953	[4]4.34	886	3/65	6/13/2011	4.88	627
258	06326500	Powder River near Locate, Montana	13,068	02/1943	[4]11.23	31,000	5/74	5/21/2011	11.70	24,100
259	06327500	Yellowstone River at Glendive, Montana	66,739	06/1909	12.70	118,000	1/20	5/23/2011	56.37	125,000
260	06329500	Yellowstone River near Sidney, Montana	68,392	06/1921	--	159,000	6/99	5/24/2011	[3,6]22.02	124,000
261	06331000	Little Muddy River below Cow Creek near Williston, North Dakota	775	04/1979	12.77	[2]9,180	2/57	4/12/2011	12.37	[2]7,470
262	06332523	East Fork Shell Creek near Parshall, North Dakota	360	03/1999	6.39	1,170	1/20	4/11/2011	7.81	3,530
263	06332770	Deepwater Creek at Mouth near Raub, North Dakota	220	03/1997	[6]13.26	[7]1,300	1/20	4/11/2011	16.10	[7]5,180
264	06334500	Little Missouri River at Camp Crook, South Dakota	1,974	04/2009	17.67	12,400	1/56	5/24/2011	19.40	20,100

Table 1. Peak streamflows at selected streamgages in the Central United States during the 2011 floods.—Continued

[mi², square miles; ft, feet; ft³/s, cubic feet per second; --, data not available; n/a, not applicable]

Map site number (fig. 4)	Station number	Station name	Contributing drainage area (mi²)	Previous maximum streamflow			Flood data			
				Date	Stage (ft)	Streamflow (ft³/s)	Rank/annual peaks in record	Date of peak streamflow	Peak stage (ft)	Peak streamflow (ft³/s)
265	06334625	Coal Creek tributary near Mill Iron, Montana	0.6	06/1991	6.64	205	4/38	5/10/2011	3.42	48
266	06335500	Little Missouri River at Marmarth, North Dakota	4,640	03/1947	21.70	45,000	3/73	5/23/2011	21.11	40,300
267	06336000	Little Missouri River at Medora, North Dakota	6,190	03/1947	20.50	65,000	5/61	5/25/2011	20.39	35,100
268	06336600	Beaver Creek near Trotters, North Dakota	616	03/1978	[5]18.61	2,720	2/34	4/3/2011	18.50	2,560
269	06337000	Little Missouri River near Watford City, North Dakota	8,310	03/1947	24.00	110,000	5/77	5/27/2011	16.70	34,000
271	06342500	Missouri River at Bismarck, North Dakota	186,400	04/1952	27.90	500,000	8/83	6/25/2011	[3]19.25	[2]155,000
274	06357800	Grand River at Little Eagle, South Dakota	5,322	03/2009	24.60	[2]32,400	5/53	3/18/2011	[3,6]21.27	[2,7]16,000
275	06359500	Moreau River near Faith, South Dakota	2,596	04/1944	[4]21.90	26,000	6/68	3/17/2011	[6]19.92	[6]17,800
276	06360500	Moreau River near Whitehorse, South Dakota	4,878	03/1997	[5]26.93	29,700	1/58	3/20/2011	26.92	34,200
277	06392900	Beaver Creek at Mallo Camp near Four Corners, Wyoming	10.3	04/1994	2.14	103	1/29	5/21/2011	2.37	154
278	06428500	Belle Fourche River at the Wyoming-South Dakota State Line	3,241	05/1995	16.33	[2]6,320	2/65	5/23/2011	16.06	[2]5,840
279	06430800	Annie Creek near Lead, South Dakota	3.7	06/2007	5.35	270	3/23	5/22/2011	5.35	109
280	06430850	Little Spearfish Creek near Lead, South Dakota	27.8	06/1999	5.79	90	2/23	5/22/2011	5.21	67
281	06436000	Belle Fourche River near Fruitdale, South Dakota	4,513	05/1982	14.32	[2]12,700	4/66	5/24/2011	13.84	[2]10,400
282	06436760	Horse Creek above Vale, South Dakota	461	05/1982	24.80	[2]17,700	3/31	5/21/2011	21.05	[2]11,100
283	06437000	Belle Fourche River near Sturgis, South Dakota	5,814	05/1982	19.10	[2]36,400	3/66	5/25/2011	17.39	[2]24,400
284	06438000	Belle Fourche River near Elm Springs, South Dakota	7,022	06/2008	19.73	[2]47,500	6/84	5/25/2011	16.09	[2]35,800

Table 1. Peak streamflows at selected streamgages in the Central United States during the 2011 floods.—Continued

[mi², square miles; ft, feet; ft³/s, cubic feet per second; --, data not available; n/a, not applicable]

Map site number (fig. 4)	Station number	Station name	Contributing drainage area (mi²)	Previous maximum streamflow			Flood data Rank[1]/annual peaks in record	Floods of 2011		
				Date	Stage (ft)	Streamflow (ft³/s)		Date of peak streamflow	Peak stage (ft)	Peak streamflow (ft³/s)
286	06441500	Bad River near Fort Pierre, South Dakota	3,147	07/1905	32.90	[7,9,14]70,000	6/86	6/21/2011	27.27	23,300
288	06452320	Platte Creek near Platte, South Dakota	747	05/1995	11.29	2,600	1/23	6/22/2011	[3]12.91	3,570
290	06468170	James River near Grace City, North Dakota	410	04/2009	17.74	7,910	1/43	4/11/2011	17.54	8,140
291	06468250	James River above Arrowwood Lake near Kensal, North Dakota	450	04/2009	[5,6]14.70	8,470	2/26	4/12/2011	14.41	7,800
292	06469400	Pipestem Creek near Pingree, North Dakota	260	04/2009	13.15	9,200	2/38	4/9/2011	[3]12.33	3,680
293	06470000	James River at Jamestown, North Dakota	1,170	05/1950	15.82	6,390	5/77	9/20/2011	13.01	[2]2,470
294	06470500	James River at Lamoure, North Dakota	1,790	04/2009	17.56	[2]12,200	5/62	7/1/2011	[3,6]14.48	[2]4,600
295	06470800	Bear Creek near Oakes, North Dakota	102	04/2009	[5]12.25	1,900	1/35	4/6/2011	12.90	2,570
296	06470878	James River at North Dakota-South Dakota State Line	2,180	04/2009	96.35	[2]11,800	2/10	4/12/2011	[3,6]95.63	28,070
297	06471000	James River at Columbia, South Dakota	4,961	04/2009	[6]19.73	[2]9,620	2/66	7/17/2011	[3,6]19.79	[2]6,200
298	06472000	James River near Stratford, South Dakota	7,647	04/2009	19.98	9,910	2/38	4/29/2011	[3,6]21.57	9,460
299	06473000	James River at Ashton, South Dakota	8,326	04/2009	[5,6]23.03	9,500	1/66	5/2/2011	[3,6]24.40	9,520
300	06475000	James River near Redfield, South Dakota	11,869	04/1997	29.92	17,000	3/62	4/27/2011	28.09	12,700
301	06476000	James River at Huron, South Dakota	13,743	04/1997	21.28	23,400	2/72	3/26/2011	[6]20.07	19,900
302	06477000	James River near Forestburg, South Dakota	15,549	04/1997	20.61	25,600	1/62	3/25/2011	20.27	28,400
303	06477500	Firesteel Creek near Mount Vernon, South Dakota	587	07/2010	16.04	7,420	6/56	3/17/2011	[3]13.86	4,720
304	06478000	James River near Mitchell, South Dakota	17,023	04/1997	[4]23.14	[9]28,000	1/25	3/25/2011	25.20	28,400
305	06478500	James River near Scotland, South Dakota	18,601	06/1984	20.45	29,400	2/83	3/27/2011	19.52	28,400

Table 1   39

Table 1. Peak streamflows at selected streamgages in the Central United States during the 2011 floods.—Continued

[mi², square miles; ft, feet; ft³/s, cubic feet per second; --, data not available; n/a, not applicable]

Map site number (fig. 4)	Station number	Station name	Contributing drainage area (mi²)	Previous maximum streamflow			Flood data Rank[1] annual peaks in record	Floods of 2011		
				Date	Stage (ft)	Streamflow (ft³/s)		Date of peak streamflow	Peak stage (ft)	Peak streamflow (ft³/s)
306	06478513	James River near Yankton, South Dakota	18,891	04/1997	22.94	28,800	1/25	3/28/2011	22.24	29,200
307	06480000	Big Sioux River near Brookings, South Dakota	2,469	04/1969	14.77	33,900	3/58	3/24/2011	13.33	15,400
308	06481000	Big Sioux River near Dell Rapids, South Dakota	3,057	04/1969	16.47	41,300	9/63	3/24/2011	[6]15.63	13,600
309	06482020	Big Sioux River at North Cliff Ave at Sioux Falls, South Dakota	3,778	04/1969	27.45	[2,9]40,700	9/41	3/25/2011	21.53	[2]13,300
311	06486000	Missouri River at Sioux City, Iowa	314,600	04/1952	[4]24.28	441,000	4/76	7/20/2011	[3]35.25	[2]192,000
313	06601200	Missouri River at Decatur, Nebraska	316,200	04/1997	31.99	[2]100,000	1/23	6/28/2011	[3]40.24	[2]191,000
315	06610000	Missouri River at Omaha, Nebraska	322,800	04/1952	[4]30.20	396,000	2/83	7/2/2011	36.29	[2]217,000
316	06614800	Michigan River near Cameron Pass, Colorado	1.5	07/1995	3.69	115	4/38	7/8/2011	3.80	90
317	06622700	North Brush Creek near Saratoga, Wyoming	37.4	06/2010	5.38	1,360	1/52	7/19/2011	5.83	1,550
318	06623800	Encampment River above Hog Park Creek near Encampment, Wyoming	72.7	06/2010	6.18	2,280	2/47	6/30/2011	6.06	2,180
319	06630000	North Platte River above Seminoe Reservoir near Sinclair, Wyoming	4,061	06/2010	11.64	[2]16,700	2/72	6/9/2011	11.46	[2]16,200
320	06657000	North Platte River below Whalen Diversion Dam, Wyoming	15,018	06/1955	[4]9.85	22,000	17/96	6/22/2011	10.31	[2]7,210
321	06674500	North Platte River at Wyoming-Nebraska State Line	22,218	06/1929	[4]6.04	[2]17,900	8/83	6/11/2011	6.45	[2]8,050
322	06715000	Clear Creek above West Fork Clear Creek near Empire, Colorado	86.3	06/1995	6.63	1,030	1/17	7/8/2011	6.46	1,060
323	06727500	Fourmile Creek at Orodell, Colorado	24.2	06/1991	[4]4.38	256	1/20	7/13/2011	9.80	770
324	06746110	Joe Wright Creek below Joe Wright Reservoir, Colorado	6.9	08/1991	2.71	[2]284	1/34	6/30/2011	2.83	[2]301
328	06807000	Missouri River at Nebraska City, Nebraska	410,000	04/1952	[4,5]24.48	414,000	2/82	7/7/2011	[3]28.27	[2]229,000
330	06813500	Missouri River at Rulo, Nebraska	414,900	04/1952	25.60	358,000	2/62	6/27/2011	27.26	[2]328,000

Table 1   41

Table 1. Peak streamflows at selected streamgages in the Central United States during the 2011 floods.—Continued

[mi², square miles; ft, feet; ft³/s, cubic feet per second; --, data not available; n/a, not applicable]

Map site number (fig. 4)	Station number	Station name	Contributing drainage area (mi²)	Previous maximum streamflow			Rank/ annual peaks in record	Floods of 2011		
				Date	Stage (ft)	Streamflow (ft³/s)		Date of peak streamflow	Peak stage (ft)	Peak streamflow (ft³/s)
332	06817000	Nodaway River at Clarinda, Iowa	762	06/2008	26.61	47,900	5/85	6/27/2011	22.98	30,000
333	06818000	Missouri River at St. Joseph, Missouri	426,500	04/1952	26.82	[2]397,000	5/93	6/28/2011	29.97	[2]277,000
334	06819110	Middle Branch 102 River near Gravity, Iowa	34.5	06/2010	70.29	7,100	1/46	5/11/2011	70.31	7,130
335	06853800	White Rock Creek near Burr Oak, Kansas	227	09/1973	[1]25.06	15,800	3/55	5/25/2011	21.30	6,660
336	06856600	Republican River at Clay Center, Kansas	17,042	06/1935	25.74	195,000	11/96	6/2/2011	22.18	[2]29,000
337	06875900	Solomon River near Glen Elder, Kansas	5,340	07/1993	29.57	[2]9,410	4/47	6/2/2011	26.76	[2]6,100
339	06893000	Missouri River at Kansas City, Missouri	484,100	06/1844	48.00	[9]625,000	15/85	6/10/2011	32.60	[2]245,000
343	06928000	Gasconade River near Hazelgreen, Missouri	1,250	01/1916	30.60	[9,1]490,000	7/67	4/26/2011	29.87	64,300
344	06933500	Gasconade River at Jerome, Missouri	2,840	12/1982	31.34	136,000	8/93	4/27/2011	26.58	85,100
345	06934000	Gasconade River near Rich Fountain, Missouri	3,180	12/1982	33.27	[9]134,000	6/72	4/28/2011	28.65	88,000
346	06934500	Missouri River at Hermann, Missouri	522,500	07/1993	36.97	[2]750,000	45/84	5/27/2011	26.60	[2]279,000
Ohio River Basin										
354	03118000	Middle Branch Nimishillen Creek at Canton, Ohio	43.1	01/1959	6.50	2,470	2/70	3/1/2011	6.78	2,420
355	03118500	Nimishillen Creek at North Industry, Ohio	175	07/2003	14.18	9,310	3/90	2/28/2011	12.92	7,920
357	03139000	Killbuck Creek at Killbuck, Ohio	464	07/1969	26.40	47,500	5/80	3/1/2011	18.07	10,000
374	03271000	Wolf Creek at Dayton, Ohio	68.7	01/1959	[4]55.13	[7,9]12,500	4/38	4/19/2011	11.19	8,130
375	03272700	Sevenmile Creek at Camden, Ohio	69.0	05/1989	18.67	20,200	4/41	4/19/2011	14.14	9,060
378	03277200	Ohio River at Markland Dam near Warsaw, Kentucky	83,170	03/1997	60.72	[2]582,000	7/41	4/26/2011	51.97	[2]518,000
382	03291780	Indian-Kentuck Creek near Canaan, Indiana	27.5	05/1990	11.34	7,800	1/42	4/19/2011	11.60	8,300

Table 1. Peak streamflows at selected streamgages in the Central United States during the 2011 floods.—Continued

[mi², square miles; ft, feet; ft³/s, cubic feet per second; --, data not available; n/a, not applicable]

Map site number (fig. 4)	Station number	Station name	Contributing drainage area (mi²)	Previous maximum streamflow			Rank/annual peaks in record	Floods of 2011		
				Date	Stage (ft)	Streamflow (ft³/s)		Date of peak streamflow	Peak stage (ft)	Peak streamflow (ft³/s)
383	03294500	Ohio River at Louisville, Kentucky	91,170	01/1937	85.44	1,110,000	13/148	4/27/2011	62.88	[2]682,000
385	03303280	Ohio River at Cannelton Dam at Cannelton, Indiana	97,000	03/1997	52.42	[2]736,000	2/33	4/28/2011	49.30	[2,8]648,000
387	03320000	Green River at Lock 2 at Calhoun, Kentucky	6,032	01/1937	37.50	208,000	9/81	5/4/2011	[3]34.04	[2]76,900
394	03373500	East Fork White River at Shoals, Indiana	4,927	03/1913	42.20	160,000	13/109	4/26/2011	30.67	[2]64,000
395	03374000	White River at Petersburg, Indiana	11,125	03/1913	[4]29.50	[7,9]235,000	8/89	5/3/2011	26.88	[2]133,000
396	03375500	Patoka River at Jasper, Indiana	262	03/1913	[4]15.90	[2,14]16,000	16/66	5/3/2011	16.68	[2]4,550
397	03376300	Patoka River at Winslow, Indiana	603	03/1964	[5]28.84	15,500	5/38	4/27/2011	27.32	[2]11,800
398	03376500	Patoka River near Princeton, Indiana	822	01/1937	26.80	18,700	2/77	5/4/2011	24.89	[2]15,700
399	03377500	Wabash River at Mount Carmel, Illinois	28,635	03/1913	[4,5]31.00	428,000	9/131	5/3/2011	34.02	[2]270,000
400	03378550	Big Creek near Wadesville, Indiana	104	03/2008	20.55	14,300	5/46	4/24/2011	19.64	9,240
401	03380500	Skillet Fork at Wayne City, Illinois	464	05/1990	25.75	59,400	8/94	4/28/2011	22.88	22,600
402	03381500	Little Wabash River at Carmi, Illinois	3,102	05/1961	[5]36.66	[2]46,900	1/72	5/3/2011	[3]36.42	255,300
403	03381700	Ohio River at Old Shawneetown, Illinois	141,000	01/2005	50.57	1,030,000	1/9	5/6/2011	[3]56.37	1,260,000
404	03382100	South Fork Saline River near Carrier Mills, Illinois	147	03/2008	18.41	24,300	2/46	5/3/2011	16.11	7,870
405	03383000	Tradewater River at Olney, Kentucky	246	01/1937	19.27	[9,14]17,000	4/70	4/28/2011	17.74	9,610
406	03399800	Ohio River at Smithland Dam, Smithland, Kentucky	144,000	03/1997	51.44	[2,8]831,000	1/18	5/6/2011	54.83	[2,8,1]1,170,000
415	03605555	Trace Creek above Denver, Tennessee	31.9	05/2010	17.88	[7,9,10,14]14,000	4/49	4/27/2011	12.27	8,930
416	03611500	Ohio River at Metropolis, Illinois	203,000	02/1937	--	[2,8]1,850,000	4/83	5/6/2011	61.65	[2,8,1]1,280,000
417	03612000	Cache River at Forman, Illinois	244	03/2008	[5]39.01	20,400	2/88	4/27/2011	37.52	[2]11,900
		Lower Mississippi River Basin (downstream from the mouth of the Ohio River)								
418	07022300	Mississippi River near Wickliffe, Kentucky	918,500	02/1937	[3]58.18	[1,6]2,010,000	1/1	5/5/2011	--	2,070,000

Table 1. Peak streamflows at selected streamgages in the Central United States during the 2011 floods.—Continued

[mi², square miles; ft, feet; ft³/s, cubic feet per second; --, data not available; n/a, not applicable]

Map site number (fig. 4)	Station number	Station name	Contributing drainage area (mi²)	Previous maximum streamflow			Flood data — Floods of 2011			
				Date	Stage (ft)	Streamflow (ft³/s)	Rank/annual peaks in record	Date of peak streamflow	Peak stage (ft)	Peak streamflow (ft³/s)
419	07024500	South Fork Obion River near Greenfield, Tennessee	383	05/2010	[5]23.08	38,000	7/78	5/3/2011	21.76	18,200
420	07026040	Obion River at Highway 51 near Obion, Tennessee	1,875	01/1937	40.40	[9]99,500	2/68	5/6/2011	39.31	[7,8]63,900
421	07030050	Hatchie River at Rialto, Tennessee	2,308	01/1946	[15]22.90	55,700	1/47	5/3/2011	21.79	55,800
422	07030240	Loosahatchie River near Arlington, Tennessee	262	05/2010	25.44	29,600	5/42	4/28/2011	23.87	22,700
423	07030392	Wolf River at La Grange, Tennessee	210	05/2010	15.72	12,200	1/16	4/27/2011	15.88	12,800
424	07030500	Wolf River at Rossville, Tennessee	503	01/1935	13.75	40,000	3/52	4/28/2011	14.46	29,400
425	07031650	Wolf River at Germantown, Tennessee	699	03/1975	27.98	33,400	2/38	4/29/2011	26.91	28,900
426	07032000	Mississippi River at Memphis, Tennessee	932,800	02/1937	[3,17]50.40	[18]2,020,000	1/83	5/9/2011	48.03	2,190,000
427	07032200	Noncannah Creek near Germantown, Tennessee	68.2	10/2002	23.87	14,600	2/42	4/27/2011	23.48	13,800
428	07035000	Little St. Francis River at Fredericktown, Missouri	90.5	11/1993	26.50	25,100	2/23	4/26/2011	22.39	15,000
429	07036100	St. Francis River near Saco, Missouri	664	11/1993	36.10	161,000	4/20	4/26/2011	27.94	63,200
430	07037500	St. Francis River near Patterson, Missouri	956	12/1982	35.77	155,000	4/91	5/2/2011	30.92	80,000
431	07039500	St. Francis River at Wappapello, Missouri	1,311	08/1915	--	[1]485,000	2/71	5/3/2011	35.64	[2]228,100
432	07040000	St. Francis River at Fisk, Missouri	1,370	04/2008	23.33	[2]11,400	1/13	5/3/2011	27.10	[2]18,800
433	07040100	St. Francis River at St. Francis, Arkansas	1,770	03/1935	28.20	39,200	2/90	5/3/2011	[3]27.25	[2]27,000
434	07040450	St. Francis River at Lake City, Arkansas	2,370	04/1979	--	[2]42,700	2/87	5/3/2011	14.37	[2]42,600
435	07043500	Little River Ditch 1 near Morehouse, Missouri	341	02/1989	19.50	12,200	3/63	4/28/2011	19.77	10,300
436	07047800	St. Francis River at Parkin, Arkansas	[11]--	01/1930	--	[2]25,300	5/75	5/6/2011	28.02	[2]24,000
437	07047970	Mississippi River at Helena, Arkansas	941,800	04/1912	[3,17]54.30	[14]2,040,000	1/132	5/11/2011	56.59	[2]2,180,000

Table 1   43

Table 1. Peak streamflows at selected streamgages in the Central United States during the 2011 floods.—Continued

[mi², square miles; ft, feet; ft³/s, cubic feet per second; --, data not available; n/a, not applicable]

Map site number (fig. 4)	Station number	Station name	Contributing drainage area (mi²)	Previous maximum streamflow			Flood data			
				Date	Stage (ft)	Streamflow (ft³/s)	Rank[1]/annual peaks in record	Floods of 2011		
								Date of peak streamflow	Peak stage (ft)	Peak streamflow (ft³/s)
438	07050700	James River near Springfield, Missouri	246	07/1909	22.00	[9,14]62,000	4/57	4/26/2011	18.85	[2]30,600
439	07052250	James River near Boaz, Missouri	461	03/2008	23.55	[2]41,900	3/18	4/25/2011	20.82	[2]30,500
440	07052500	James River at Galena, Missouri	987	03/2008	35.96	85,100	3/90	4/26/2011	[6]30.95	64,000
441	07057500	North Fork River near Tecumseh, Missouri	561	11/1985	28.10	133,000	3/67	4/26/2011	24.58	81,000
442	07058000	Bryant Creek near Tecumseh, Missouri	570	12/1982	26.74	71,100	2/57	4/26/2011	23.01	47,600
445	07062500	Black River at Leeper, Missouri	987	03/1904	22.30	[9,14]125,000	24/79	4/24/2011	12.98	[2]11,700
446	07063000	Black River at Poplar Bluff, Missouri	1,245	03/1904	--	[7,9,14]100,000	15/90	4/26/2011	21.41	[2]24,400
447	07064000	Black River near Corning, Arkansas	1,750	06/1945	16.92	48,600	2/95	4/28/2011	18.12	[2]40,700
448	07068000	Current River at Doniphan, Missouri	2,038	03/1904	24.90	[9,14]130,000	7/95	4/26/2011	23.76	90,100
449	07069000	Black River at Pocahontas, Arkansas	4,840	04/1927	25.90	[9]80,000	1/76	4/28/2011	28.44	[2]86,600
450	07071500	Eleven Point River near Bardley, Missouri	793	12/1982	21.64	49,800	5/91	4/26/2011	17.83	33,400
451	07072500	Black River at Black Rock, Arkansas	7,370	12/1982	[7]31.51	[7]190,000	2/107	4/26/2011	30.45	172,000
452	07074420	Black River at Elgin Ferry, Arkansas	8,420	03/2008	[6]32.57	[7]127,000	1/24	4/28/2011	[3]34.77	212,000
453	07074500	White River at Newport, Arkansas	19,900	04/1945	[5,7]35.19	[2]343,000	6/126	5/4/2011	34.17	[2]292,000
454	07074850	White River near Augusta, Arkansas	20,500	03/2008	38.41	[2]252,000	1/74	5/5/2011	40.70	[2]262,000
456	07077380	Cache River at Egypt, Arkansas	701	01/1966	21.88	8,940	2/62	5/4/2011	22.15	8,500
457	07083710	Arkansas River below Empire Gulch near Malta, Colorado	238	06/2008	5.41	[2]1,530	1/12	6/17/2011	5.72	[2]1,590
458	07105800	Fountain Creek at Security, Colorado	500	07/1965	11.30	25,000	4/47	9/14/2011	9.48	13,200
459	07105900	Jimmy Camp Creek at Fountain, Colorado	65.4	06/1965	--	[7,9]124,000	4/37	9/15/2011	10.46	4,120
460	07106300	Fountain Creek near Pinon, Colorado	865	04/1999	9.80	[2]19,100	2/39	9/15/2011	9.36	[2]13,600
469	07188653	Big Sugar Creek near Powell, Missouri	141	04/2008	18.11	15,800	1/11	4/25/2011	21.99	24,000
470	07188885	Indian Creek near Lanagan, Missouri	239	03/2008	13.31	14,600	1/12	5/24/2011	14.07	16,100
471	07189100	Buffalo Creek at Tiff City, Missouri	91.6	06/2007	14.31	15,700	1/11	5/24/2011	15.28	26,300
472	07189540	Cave Springs Branch near Southwest City, Missouri	7.9	04/2008	12.45	2,470	2/14	5/23/2011	12.30	2,340

Table 1. Peak streamflows at selected streamgages in the Central United States during the 2011 floods.—Continued

[mi², square miles; ft, feet; ft³/s, cubic feet per second; --, data not available; n/a, not applicable]

Map site number (fig. 4)	Station number	Station name	Contributing drainage area (mi²)	Previous maximum streamflow			Flood data			
				Date	Stage (ft)	Streamflow (ft³/s)	Rank/annual peaks in record	Date of peak streamflow	Floods of 2011	
									Peak stage (ft)	Peak streamflow (ft³/s)
473	07189542	Honey Creek near Southwest City, Missouri	48.2	04/2008	13.89	9,210	2/14	5/24/2011	13.27	7,020
474	07191000	Big Cabin Creek near Big Cabin, Oklahoma	450	05/1943	[4]34.96	63,000	4/72	5/24/2011	48.74	[2]45,900
476	07194800	Illinois River at Savoy, Arkansas	167	04/2004	19.63	39,800	1/19	4/25/2011	[7]24.66	86,900
477	07195000	Osage Creek near Elm Springs, Arkansas	130	05/1961	16.66	22,500	1/46	4/25/2011	18.70	38,000
478	07195400	Illinois River at Highway 16 near Siloam Springs, Arkansas	509	03/2008	21.53	61,000	1/12	4/26/2011	26.23	87,100
479	07195430	Illinois River south of Siloam Springs, Arkansas	575	04/2004	20.54	52,000	1/16	4/26/2011	27.71	106,000
480	07195500	Illinois River near Watts, Oklahoma	635	07/1960	25.96	68,000	1/56	4/26/2011	28.60	[2]97,400
481	07196090	Illinois River at Chewey, Oklahoma	825	n/a	n/a	n/a	1/1	4/26/2011	29.54	92,200
482	07196500	Illinois River near Tahlequah, Oklahoma	959	05/1950	27.94	[7]150,000	4/79	4/26/2011	25.97	[2]85,400
483	07197000	Baron Fork at Eldon, Oklahoma	307	06/2000	26.77	54,700	1/65	4/25/2011	28.51	[2]63,400
484	07197360	Caney Creek near Barber, Oklahoma	89.6	06/2000	[4,5]15.67	[7,8,9]9,720	1/14	4/25/2011	[3,6]31.42	[7]13,100
485	07198000	Illinois River near Gore, Oklahoma	1,626	05/1950	[4]30.20	180,000	14/73	5/24/2011	17.57	215,900
487	07249985	Lee Creek near Short, Oklahoma	420	04/2004	[5]27.77	82,400	3/66	4/26/2011	26.08	70,100
488	07250965	Frog Bayou at Winfrey, Arkansas	54.2	04/2004	11.58	12,900	1/9	4/25/2011	13.88	21,800
489	07265450	Mississippi River at Arkansas City, Arkansas	1,130,600	05/1927	359.20	[2,14,19]2,500,000	2/88	5/17/2011	53.14	[2,7]2,400,000
490	07289000	Mississippi River at Vicksburg, Mississippi	1,140,500	05/1927	356.20	[2]2,278,000	1/91	5/17/2011	57.17	[2,8]2,310,000
492	07374000	Mississippi River at Baton Rouge, Louisiana	1,125,810	04/1945	45.18	1,473,000	2/36	5/18/2011	45.48	[2]1,440,000
493	07374525	Mississippi River at Belle Chase, Louisiana	1,110,000	02/2010	[5]15.84	1,210,000	1/3	5/17/2011	[3]18.28	1,320,000
494	07381482	Old River Outflow Channel below Hydropower Channel, Louisiana	[20]--	04/2010	[5]35.08	423,000	1/3	5/20/2011	[3]49.82	730,000

Table 1   45

Table 1. Peak streamflows at selected streamgages in the Central United States during the 2011 floods.—Continued

[mi², square miles; ft, feet; ft³/s, cubic feet per second; --, data not available; n/a, not applicable]

Map site number (fig. 4)	Station number	Station name	Contributing drainage area (mi²)	Previous maximum streamflow			Flood data	Floods of 2011		
				Date	Stage (ft)	Streamflow (ft³/s)	Rank[1]/annual peaks in record	Date of peak streamflow	Peak stage (ft)	Peak streamflow (ft³/s)
495	07381490	Atchafalaya River at Simmesport, Louisiana	[20]--	05/1973	53.40	781,000	3/9	5/24/2011	45.06	697,000
496	07381590	Wax Lake Outlet at Calumet, Louisiana	[20]--	04/1997	--	[8]258,000	1/67	5/27/2011	10.81	323,000
497	07381600	Lower Atchafalaya River at Morgan City, Louisiana	[20]--	04/2008	[5]7.81	366,000	1/34	5/29/2011	[3]10.33	512,000

[1]Rank of the maximum instantaneous peak streamflow measured during 2011 event compared to all systematic and historic annual peaks. A rank of 1 indicates that the 2011 peak streamflow was higher than all other recorded annual peaks.

[2]Streamflow was affected by regulation or diversion.

[3]Stage corresponds to maximum stage for the flood, not the stage when the peak streamflow occurred.

[4]Gage height was measured at a different site or datum (or both) than the 2011 peak.

[5]Stage is the stage of peak flow, not the maximum historic stage.

[6]Stage is affected by backwater.

[7]Estimated.

[8]Streamflow is a maximum daily average. Peak streamflow may be higher.

[9]Streamflow is an historic peak.

[10]Streamflow is unknown but greater than the reported value.

[11]All or part of the record is affected by urbanization, mining, agricultural changes, channelization, or other.

[12]Streamflow was affected by dam failure.

[13]No USGS streamgage is currently in operation at this site. Streamflow is provided by AmerenUE and computed from operation of turbines in power plant and spillway gates at dam.

[14]Month or day of occurrence is unknown or not exact.

[15]A previous historic peak stage and unknown streamflow exists that likely exceeds the previous max streamflow.

[16]This value is for Hickman, Kentucky which is 29.6 river miles downstream from Wickliffe, Kentucky and includes the flow through the New Madrid Floodway (Mississippi River Commission, 1955). The 1912 and 1913 maximum discharges were 2,015,000 ft³/s (Mississippi River Commission, 1955).

[17]Source: Mississippi River Commission, 1954, Annual highest and lowest stages of the Mississippi River and its outlets and tributaries to 1953, Vicksburg, Mississippi, 253 p.

[18]Source: Mississippi River Commission, 1955, Annual maximum minimum and mean discharges of the Mississippi River and its outlets and tributaries to 1953, Vicksburg, Mississippi, 140 p.

[19]The amount of flow actually measured was 1,712,000 ft³/s (Mississippi River Commission, 1955), but 2,500,000 ft³/s was the estimated total flow past Arkansas City factoring in that flow which was bypassing the main channel area through the ruptured levees (written commun., 2012, Charles Shade, Chief, Water Control, Mississippi Valley Division, U.S. Army Corps of Engineers).

[20]Major river diversions upstream cause these drainage areas to be indeterminate.

Table 2   47

Table 2.   Annual runoff volumes at selected streamgages in the Central United States during water year 2011.

[mi², square miles; <, less than; >, greater than]

Map site number (fig. 4)	Station number	Station name	Contributing drainage area (mi²)	Period of record: Water years with streamflow data	Period of record: Number of years with streamflow data	Period of record: Median annual runoff (acre-feet)	Mean annual runoff (acre-feet)	Previous maximum annual runoff based on data through water year 2010[1]: Water year	Previous maximum annual runoff based on data through water year 2010[1]: Annual runoff (acre-feet)	Water year 2011: Rank	Water year 2011: Annual runoff (acre-feet)
		Red River of the North Basin									
2	05046000	Otter Tail River below Orwell Dam near Fergus Falls, Minnesota	1,740	1931–2011	81	255,600	295,700	2009	679,100	1	1,050,000
4	05050000	Bois De Sioux River near White Rock, South Dakota	1,160	1942–2011	70	59,000	100,300	1997	388,100	1	607,400
5	05051500	Red River of the North at Wahpeton, North Dakota	4,010	1944–2011	68	453,600	531,000	2009	1,332,000	1	2,005,000
9	05053000	Wild Rice River near Abercrombie, North Dakota	1,490	1933–2011	79	41,270	106,400	2009	697,200	1	854,300
10	05054000	Red River of the North at Fargo, North Dakota	6,800	1902–2011	110	417,400	580,800	2009	2,527,000	1	3,214,000
12	05056000	Sheyenne River near Warwick, North Dakota	760	1950–2011	62	44,890	62,890	2009	272,900	1	345,300
22	05059500	Sheyenne River at West Fargo, North Dakota	3,090	1904–05, 1930–2011	84	133,900	199,300	2010	752,900	1	1,267,000
27	05062000	Buffalo River near Dilworth, Minnesota	975	1932–2011	80	108,200	131,900	2009	526,300	2	460,400
28	05064000	Wild Rice River at Hendrum, Minnesota	1,560	1945–84, 1986–2011	66	228,800	268,500	2009	738,500	1	760,200
31	05066500	Goose River at Hillsboro, North Dakota	1,093	1932, 1935–2011	78	44,890	83,450	2009	298,300	1	485,800
32	05069000	Sand Hill River at Climax, Minnesota	420	1947–84, 1986–2011	64	60,810	67,650	1999	180,300	1	186,800
35	05079000	Red Lake River at Crookston, Minnesota	5,270	1902–2011	110	810,900	893,000	1950	2,266,000	4	1,911,000
36	05082500	Red River of the North at Grand Forks, North Dakota	26,300	1905–2011	107	1,911,000	2,405,000	2009	7,964,000	1	10,350,000
38	05085000	Forest River at Minto, North Dakota	620	1945–2011	67	35,470	43,230	2009	198,400	7	96,290
39	05087500	Middle River at Argyle, Minnesota	255	1951–81, 1983–2011	60	34,030	41,270	1999	143,300	3	113,700
40	05090000	Park River at Grafton, North Dakota	695	1932–2011	80	40,900	51,400	2009	259,900	4	144,800

Table 2. Annual runoff volumes at selected streamgages in the Central United States during water year 2011.—Continued

[mi², square miles; <, less than; >, greater than]

Map site number (fig. 4)	Station number	Station name	Contributing drainage area (mi²)	Period of record				Previous maximum annual runoff based on data through water year 2010[1]		Water year 2011	
				Water years with streamflow data	Number of years with streamflow data	Median annual runoff (acre-feet)	Mean annual runoff (acre-feet)	Water year	Annual runoff (acre-feet)	Rank	Annual runoff (acre-feet)
41	05092000	Red River of the North at Drayton, North Dakota	34,800	1950–2011	62	3,334,000	3,570,000	2009	9,846,000	1	11,150,000
42	05094000	South Branch Two Rivers at Lake Bronson, Minnesota	422	1929–36, 1942–43, 1946–47, 1954–81, 1986–2011	66	54,300	83,420	2009	237,500	2	231,700
44	05100000	Pembina River at Neche, North Dakota	3,410	1904–08, 1910–15, 1920–2011	103	115,100	189,700	1995	810,900	1	1,050,000
45	05102500	Red River at Emerson, Manitoba	40,200	1913–2011	99	2,324,000	3,184,000	2009	10,930,000	1	12,810,000
		Souris River Basin									
46	05113600	Long Creek near Noonan, North Dakota	630	1960–2011	52	15,200	35,350	1976	145,500	1	390,200
47	05114000	Souris River near Sherwood, North Dakota	3,040	1931–2011	81	45,610	106,900	1976	637,100	1	1,643,000
49	05116500	Des Lacs River at Foxholm, North Dakota	539	1905–06, 1946–2011	68	10,860	22,260	1976	107,100	1	219,400
50	05117500	Souris River above Minot, North Dakota	3,900	1904–2011	108	60,450	127,700	1976	803,600	1	1,969,000
52	05120500	Wintering River near Karlsruhe, North Dakota	285	1938–2011	74	9,050	13,000	1999	59,370	1	91,220
54	05123400	Willow Creek near Willow City, North Dakota	730	1957–2011	55	15,100	42,060	1999	233,800	1	250,500
56	05124000	Souris River near Westhope, North Dakota	6,600	1931–2011	81	105,000	237,000	1976	1,231,000	1	3,403,000
		Upper Mississippi River Basin (upstream of the mouth of the Ohio River), excluding the Missouri River Basin									
57	05211000	Mississippi River at Grand Rapids, Minnesota	3,370	1886–88, 1901–03, 1905–09, 1912–37, 1939–2011	110	890,500	898,700	1906	1,759,000	11	1,506,000

Table 2   49

Table 2. Annual runoff volumes at selected streamgages in the Central United States during water year 2011.—Continued

[mi², square miles; <, less than; >, greater than]

Map site number (fig. 4)	Station number	Station name	Contributing drainage area (mi²)	Period of record				Previous maximum annual runoff based on data through water year 2010[1]		Water year 2011	
				Water years with stream-flow data	Number of years with streamflow data	Median annual runoff (acre-feet)	Mean annual runoff (acre-feet)	Water year	Annual runoff (acre-feet)	Rank	Annual runoff (acre-feet)
58	05244000	Crow Wing River at Nimrod, Minnesota	1,030	1940–81, 1992–2011	62	360,500	349,100	1999	548,000	4	475,600
59	05267000	Mississippi River near Royalton, Minnesota	11,600	1925–2011	87	3,388,000	3,524,000	1966	6,921,000	6	5,756,000
60	05270500	Sauk River near St. Cloud, Minnesota	1,030	1910–12, 1931, 1935–81, 1991–2011	72	233,800	238,300	1972	530,700	1	752,900
62	05280000	Crow River at Rockford, Minnesota	2,640	1910–11, 1913–17, 1931, 1935–2011	85	521,300	632,900	1986	1,991,000	1	2,367,000
63	05286000	Rum River near St. Francis, Minnesota	1,360	1931, 1934–2011	79	461,200	471,000	1986	1,093,000	2	1,021,000
65	05288500	Mississippi River near Anoka, Minnesota	19,100	1932–2011	80	5,998,000	6,064,000	1986	12,810,000	2	11,730,000
67	05292000	Minnesota River at Ortonville, Minnesota	1,160	1939–2011	73	72,400	112,600	2010	453,200	1	530,700
69	05294000	Pomme De Terre River at Appleton, Minnesota	905	1936–99, 2004–11	72	78,190	107,900	1997	304,100	1	490,100
70	05300000	Lac Qui Parle River near Lac Qui Parle, Minnesota	960	1913, 1932, 1934–99, 2002–11	78	92,670	125,900	1993	452,500	1	553,100
72	05311000	Minnesota River at Montevideo, Minnesota	6,180	1910–17, 1930–2011	90	530,700	727,400	1997	2,295,000	1	3,337,000
76	05317000	Cottonwood River near New Ulm, Minnesota	1,300	1912–13, 1936–37, 1939–2011	77	202,700	298,100	1993	1,303,000	2	1,187,000
78	05320000	Blue Earth River near Rapidan, Minnesota	2,410	1940–45, 1950–2011	68	721,800	827,500	1993	3,272,000	2	2,186,000

Table 2. Annual runoff volumes at selected streamgages in the Central United States during water year 2011.—Continued

[mi², square miles; <, less than; >, greater than]

Map site number (fig. 4)	Station number	Station name	Contributing drainage area (mi²)	Period of record			Mean annual runoff (acre-feet)	Previous maximum annual runoff based on data through water year 2010[1]		Water year 2011	
				Water years with streamflow data	Number of years with streamflow data	Median annual runoff (acre-feet)		Water year	Annual runoff (acre-feet)	Rank	Annual runoff (acre-feet)
81	05320500	Le Sueur River near Rapidan, Minnesota	1,110	1940–45, 1950–2011	68	413,400	420,600	1993	1,477,000	3	1,035,000
82	05325000	Minnesota River at Mankato, Minnesota	14,900	1905, 1911–17, 1930–2011	90	2,237,000	2,801,000	1993	10,790,000	1	11,000,000
83	05330000	Minnesota River near Jordan, Minnesota	16,200	1935–2011	77	2,744,000	3,476,000	1993	12,240,000	1	12,740,000
84	05331000	Mississippi River at Saint Paul, Minnesota	36,800	1895, 1897, 1901–05, 1907–2011	112	8,579,000	8,845,000	1986	21,430,000	1	26,500,000
85	05340500	St. Croix River at St. Croix Falls, Wisconsin	6,240	1911–2011	101	3,178,000	3,175,000	1986	6,204,000	5	4,793,000
86	05344500	Mississippi River at Prescott, Wisconsin	44,800	1929–2011	83	13,830,000	13,600,000	1986	27,870,000	1	31,560,000
88	05355200	Cannon River at Welch, Minnesota	1,340	1912–13, 1932–71, 1992–2011	62	431,100	479,600	1993	1,542,000	2	1,281,000
89	05369500	Chippewa River at Durand, Wisconsin	9,010	1929–2011	83	5,640,000	5,540,000	1942	8,398,000	10	7,030,000
90	05378500	Mississippi River at Winona, Minnesota	59,200	1929–2011	83	21,570,000	21,650,000	1986	41,120,000	1	42,860,000
91	05382000	Black River near Galesville, Wisconsin	2,080	1933–2011	79	1,303,000	1,283,000	1993	2,505,000	9	1,832,000
92	05389500	Mississippi River at McGregor, Iowa	67,500	1937–2005, 2008–11	73	28,020,000	27,330,000	1993	46,840,000	1	49,950,000
94	05398000	Wisconsin River at Rothschild, Wisconsin	4,020	1945–2011	67	2,490,000	2,511,000	1973	4,308,000	15	3,077,000
95	05407000	Wisconsin River at Muscoda, Wisconsin	10,400	1914–2011	98	6,277,000	6,293,000	1973	11,580,000	8	8,326,000
96	05412500	Turkey River at Garber, Iowa	1,545	1914–16, 1920–27, 1930–2011	91	718,900	754,900	1993	2,107,000	18	1,057,000
102	05420500	Mississippi River at Clinton, Iowa	85,600	1874–2011	138	35,730,000	35,720,000	1882	68,560,000	3	65,300,000
103	05422000	Wapsipinicon River near De Witt, Iowa	2,336	1935–2011	77	1,158,000	1,267,000	1993	3,953,000	21	1,643,000

Table 2   51

Table 2. Annual runoff volumes at selected streamgages in the Central United States during water year 2011.—Continued

[mi², square miles; <, less than; >, greater than]

Map site number (fig. 4)	Station number	Station name	Contributing drainage area (mi²)	Period of record				Previous maximum annual runoff based on data through water year 2010[1]		Water year 2011	
				Water years with streamflow data	Number of years with streamflow data	Median annual runoff (acre-feet)	Mean annual runoff (acre-feet)	Water year	Annual runoff (acre-feet)	Rank	Annual runoff (acre-feet)
104	05430500	Rock River at Afton, Wisconsin	3,340	1915–2011	97	1,376,000	1,460,000	2008	3,598,000	13	2,208,000
105	05437500	Rock River at Rockton, Illinois	6,363	1904–05, 1915–19, 1940–2011	79	3,026,000	3,254,000	2008	7,124,000	16	4,213,000
106	05446500	Rock River near Joslin, Illinois	9,549	1940–2011	72	4,608,000	4,973,000	1993	10,570,000	14	6,581,000
108	05454500	Iowa River at Iowa City, Iowa	3,271	1904–2011	108	1,256,000	1,425,000	1993	6,154,000	25	1,911,000
109	05458500	Cedar River at Janesville, Iowa	1,661	1905–06, 1915–27, 1933–42, 1946–2011	91	626,200	729,000	1993	2,498,000	8	1,325,000
110	05464500	Cedar River at Cedar Rapids, Iowa	6,510	1903–2011	109	2,585,000	2,873,000	1993	10,930,000	10	4,742,000
112	05465500	Iowa River at Wapello, Iowa	12,500	1915–2011	97	5,263,000	5,809,000	1993	22,150,000	18	8,326,000
116	05476000	Des Moines River at Jackson, Minnesota	1,250	1936–2011	76	216,500	307,600	1993	1,520,000	2	1,267,000
117	05479000	East Fork Des Moines River at Dakota City, Iowa	1,308	1941–2011	71	396,700	481,400	1993	1,984,000	7	955,600
118	05480500	Des Moines River at Fort Dodge, Iowa	4,190	1914–27, 1947–2011	79	1,173,000	1,374,000	1993	5,705,000	5	3,417,000
119	05484500	Raccoon River at Van Meter, Iowa	3,441	1916–2011	96	962,900	1,191,000	1993	4,141,000	22	1,622,000
120	05485500	Des Moines River below Racoon River at Des Moines, Iowa	9,879	1941–2011	71	3,461,000	3,851,000	1993	13,900,000	8	6,277,000
125	05490500	Des Moines River at Keosauqua, Iowa	14,038	1904–05, 1912–2011	102	4,130,000	4,971,000	1993	19,470,000	7	9,846,000
128	05526000	Iroquois River near Chebanse, Illinois	2,091	1924–2011	88	1,274,000	1,303,000	1993	3,243,000	40	1,332,000
129	05527500	Kankakee River near Wilmington, Illinois	5,150	1916–33, 1936–2011	94	3,189,000	3,316,000	1993	7,529,000	39	3,547,000
130	05543500	Illinois River at Marseilles, Illinois	8,259	1920–2011	92	7,674,000	7,817,000	1993	12,960,000	35	8,108,000
131	05552500	Fox River at Dayton, Illinois	2,642	1916–2011	96	1,372,000	1,366,000	1993	2,852,000	13	1,897,000
132	05555300	Vermilion River near Leonore, Illinois	1,251	1932–2011	80	628,100	653,300	1993	1,752,000	32	691,400

Table 2. Annual runoff volumes at selected streamgages in the Central United States during water year 2011.—Continued

[mi², square miles; <, less than; >, greater than]

Map site number (fig. 4)	Station number	Station name	Contributing drainage area (mi²)	Period of record				Previous maximum annual runoff based on data through water year 2010[1]		Water year 2011	
				Water years with streamflow data	Number of years with streamflow data	Median annual runoff (acre-feet)	Mean annual runoff (acre-feet)	Water year	Annual runoff (acre-feet)	Rank	Annual runoff (acre-feet)
133	05568500	Illinois River at Kingston Mines, Illinois	15,818	1940–2011	72	11,440,000	11,640,000	1993	23,310,000	20	13,470,000
134	05570000	Spoon River at Seville, Illinois	1,636	1915–2011	97	760,200	825,500	1993	2,592,000	16	1,187,000
135	05576500	Sangamon River at Riverton, Illinois	2,618	1909–12, 1915–56, 1987–2011	71	1,318,000	1,332,000	1927	3,482,000	15	1,962,000
136	05582000	Salt Creek near Greenview, Illinois	1,804	1942–2011	70	984,600	1,020,000	1993	2,433,000	31	1,071,000
137	05583000	Sangamon River near Oakford, Illinois	5,093	1910–11, 1915–18, 1922, 1929–33, 1940–2011	84	2,563,000	2,624,000	2010	6,545,000	22	3,497,000
138	05586100	Illinois River at Valley City, Illinois	26,743	1939–2011	73	16,290,000	16,970,000	1993	33,880,000	15	21,140,000
141	05592500	Kaskaskia River at Vandalia, Illinois	1,940	1909–12, 1915–2011	101	1,108,000	1,132,000	1927	2,614,000	13	1,759,000
143	05595000	Kaskaskia River at New Athens, Illinois	5,189	1910–12, 1915–21, 1935–71, 2010–11	49	2,795,000	2,728,000	1950	5,893,000	3	4,887,000
144	05597000	Big Muddy River at Plumfield, Illinois	794	1909, 1912, 1915–2011	99	544,400	523,100	1950	1,325,000	4	991,800
146	07010000	Mississippi River at St. Louis, Missouri	697,000	1863–2011	149	131,800,000	135,500,000	1993	311,300,000	5	233,800,000
147	07019000	Meramec River near Eureka, Missouri	3,788	1904–05, 1922–2011	92	2,299,000	2,379,000	1985	5,365,000	23	3,026,000
148	07020500	Mississippi River at Chester, Illinois	708,600	1943–2011	69	145,500,000	153,200,000	1993	320,000,000	4	244,700,000
149	07022000	Mississippi River at Thebes, Illinois	713,200	1934–37, 1940–2011	76	148,400,000	154,100,000	1993	322,900,000	3	260,600,000

Table 2   53

Table 2. Annual runoff volumes at selected streamgages in the Central United States during water year 2011.—Continued

[mi², square miles; <, less than; >, greater than]

Map site number (fig. 4)	Station number	Station name	Contributing drainage area (mi²)	Period of record				Previous maximum annual runoff based on data through water year 2010[1]		Water year 2011	
				Water years with streamflow data	Number of years with streamflow data	Median annual runoff (acre-feet)	Mean annual runoff (acre-feet)	Water year	Annual runoff (acre-feet)	Rank	Annual runoff (acre-feet)
		Missouri River Basin									
161	06036650	Jefferson River near Three Forks, Montana	9,532	1895, 1897–1898, 1900–1905, 1939–1969, 1979–2011	72	1,473,000	1,457,000	1984	2,643,000	4	2,208,000
165	06041000	Madison River below Ennis Lake near McAllister, Montana	2,186	1939–2011	73	1,216,000	1,271,000	1997	1,832,000	19	1,470,000
167	06052500	Gallatin River at Logan, Montana	1,795	1894–1905, 1929–2011	95	760,200	770,100	1997	1,209,000	6	1,137,000
168	06054500	Missouri River at Toston, Montana	14,669	1911–16, 1942–2011	76	3,660,000	3,705,000	1997	5,604,000	7	5,010,000
177	06089000	Sun River near Vaughn, Montana	1,849	1935–2011	77	469,100	486,900	1943	948,400	6	818,100
180	06090800	Missouri River at Fort Benton, Montana	24,749	1891–2011	121	5,459,000	5,511,000	1894	8,615,000	1	8,833,000
183	06101500	Marias River near Chester, Montana	4,927	1946–47, 1956–2011	58	540,400	579,200	1959	1,079,000	11	832,600
189	06115200	Missouri River near Landusky, Montana	40,987	1935–2011	77	6,349,000	6,510,000	1975	11,080,000	2	10,710,000
199	06130500	Musselshell River at Mosby, Montana	7,846	1931–32, 1935–2011	79	129,600	199,200	1978	789,100	1	1,419,000
201	06132000	Missouri River below Fort Peck Dam, Montana	57,556	1935–2000, 2002–2011	76	6,085,000	6,393,000	1975	10,860,000	1	12,810,000
210	06174500	Milk River at Nashua, Montana	22,332	1940–2011	72	380,100	475,800	1952	1,716,000	1	2,483,000
213	06185500	Missouri River near Culbertson, Montana	91,557	1942–1951, 1959–2011	63	6,653,000	7,220,000	1975	12,020,000	1	16,650,000
218	06192500	Yellowstone River near Livingston, Montana	3,551	1898–1905, 1929–1932, 1938–2011	86	2,632,000	2,713,000	1997	4,431,000	2	4,134,000
222	06207500	Clarks Fork Yellowstone River near Belfry, Montana	1,154	1922–2011	90	648,300	676,200	1997	1,079,000	4	1,014,000

Table 2. Annual runoff volumes at selected streamgages in the Central United States during water year 2011.—Continued

[mi², square miles; <, less than; >, greater than]

Map site number (fig. 4)	Station number	Station name	Contributing drainage area (mi²)	Period of record Water years with streamflow data	Period of record Number of years with streamflow data	Period of record Median annual runoff (acre-feet)	Period of record Mean annual runoff (acre-feet)	Previous maximum annual runoff based on data through water year 2010[1] Water year	Previous maximum annual runoff based on data through water year 2010[1] Annual runoff (acre-feet)	Water year 2011 Rank	Water year 2011 Annual runoff (acre-feet)
227	06214500	Yellowstone River at Billings, Montana	11,408	1929–2011	83	5,090,000	5,027,000	1997	8,760,000	2	8,181,000
239	06289000	Little Bighorn River at State line near Wyola, Montana	182	1940–2011	72	103,900	108,000	1975	183,200	2	173,000
255	06308500	Tongue River at Miles City, Montana	5,397	1939–41, 1947–2011	68	291,400	296,300	1978	713,800	2	711,700
256	06309000	Yellowstone River at Miles City, Montana	48,253	1923, 1929–2011	84	8,507,000	8,177,000	1997	12,670,000	1	14,330,000
258	06326500	Powder River near Locate, Montana	13,068	1939–2011	73	396,000	412,900	1944	1,180,000	3	948,400
260	06329500	Yellowstone River near Sidney, Montana	68,392	1911–31, 1934–2011	99	9,339,000	9,027,000	1924	15,420,000	1	16,000,000
269	06337000	Little Missouri River near Watford City, North Dakota	8,310	1935–2011	77	329,400	400,900	1971	1,187,000	1	1,477,000
270	06340500	Knife River at Hazen, North Dakota	2,240	1930–33, 1938–2011	78	99,180	122,100	2009	373,600	2	345,300
271	06342500	Missouri River at Bismarck, North Dakota	186,400	1929–2011	83	15,350,000	16,060,000	1975	25,770,000	1	38,520,000
272	06349000	Heart River at Mandan, North Dakota	3,310	1929–32, 1938–2011	78	140,100	195,200	2009	687,100	2	676,200
273	06354000	Cannonball River at Breien, North Dakota	4,100	1935–2011	77	124,500	181,000	2009	738,500	5	572,700
274	06357800	Grand River at Little Eagle, South Dakota	5,322	1959–2011	53	128,100	192,900	2009	818,100	3	573,400
275	06359500	Moreau River near Faith, South Dakota	2,596	1944–2011	68	68,780	107,000	2009	411,900	4	351,100
285	06438500	Cheyenne River near Plainview, South Dakota	21,414	1951–1981, 1995–2011	48	468,800	573,200	1997	1,752,000	3	1,578,000
287	06452000	White River near Oacoma, South Dakota	9,859	1929–2011	83	372,800	425,700	1942	1,252,000	3	1,122,000
289	06465500	Niobrara River near Verdel, Nebraska	11,580	1939, 1959–2011	54	1,166,000	1,269,000	2010	1,976,000	2	1,853,000
294	06470500	James River at LaMoure, North Dakota	1,790	1951–2011	61	78,190	151,600	2009	810,900	1	1,050,000
305	06478500	James River near Scotland, South Dakota	18,601	1929–2011	83	254,800	558,100	2010	4,214,000	2	4,199,000

Table 2   55

Table 2.   Annual runoff volumes at selected streamgages in the Central United States during water year 2011.—Continued

[mi², square miles; <, less than; >, greater than]

Map site number (fig. 4)	Station number	Station name	Contributing drainage area (mi²)	Period of record				Previous maximum annual runoff based on data through water year 2010[1]		Water year 2011	
				Water years with stream-flow data	Number of years with streamflow data	Median annual runoff (acre-feet)	Mean annual runoff (acre-feet)	Water year	Annual runoff (acre-feet)	Rank	Annual runoff (acre-feet)
310	06485500	Big Sioux River at Akron, Iowa	6,996	1929–2011	83	760,200	995,300	1993	4,539,000	2	4,214,000
311	06486000	Missouri River at Sioux City, Iowa	314,600	1929–31, 1939–2011	76	20,600,000	21,720,000	1997	40,470,000	1	57,270,000
312	06600500	Floyd River at James, Iowa	886	1936–2011	76	150,900	198,300	1983	693,600	5	607,400
314	06607500	Little Sioux River near Turin, Iowa	3,526	1943–57, 1959–2011	68	894,100	961,800	1993	3,808,000	5	2,382,000
321	06674500	North Platte River at Wyoming-Nebraska State Line	22,218	1930–2011	82	444,500	568,400	1984	2,078,000	1	2,172,000
325	06774000	Platte River near Ducan, Nebraska	54,630	1930–2011	82	991,800	1,255,000	1984	4,822,000	3	3,258,000
326	06793000	Loup River near Genoa, Nebraska	5,620	1930–31, 1944–2011	70	494,500	583,900	1930	1,976,000	19	718,900
327	06796000	Platte River at North Bend, Nebraska	57,800	1950–2011	62	3,077,000	3,308,000	1984	7,312,000	7	4,959,000
329	06810000	Nishnabotna River above Hamburg, Iowa	2,806	1923, 1929–2011	84	810,900	965,800	1993	3,663,000	13	1,455,000
330	06813500	Missouri River at Rulo, Nebraska	414,900	1950–2011	62	29,320,000	31,340,000	1997	52,050,000	1	72,400,000
331	06815000	Big Nemaha River at Falls City, Nebraska	1,339	1945–2011	67	353,300	437,600	1993	1,853,000	47	207,800
333	06818000	Missouri River at St. Joseph, Missouri	426,500	1929–2011	83	29,030,000	31,540,000	1997	55,020,000	1	75,290,000
338	06892350	Kansas River at De Soto, Kansas	59,756	1918–2011	94	4,554,000	5,325,000	1993	22,150,000	55	4,047,000
340	06902000	Grand River near Sumner, Missouri	6,880	1925–2011	87	2,795,000	3,120,000	1993	12,600,000	46	2,773,000
341	06905500	Chariton River near Prairie Hill, Missouri	1,870	1930–2011	82	850,700	959,500	2010	3,301,000	21	1,318,000
342	06926000	Osage River near Bagnell, Missouri	14,000	1926–2011	86	7,385,000	7,653,000	1927	17,810,000	46	6,914,000
346	06934500	Missouri River at Hermann, Missouri	522,500	1929–2011	83	57,270,000	59,430,000	1993	131,800,000	5	100,600,000
		Ohio River Basin									
347	03016000	Allegheny River at West Hickory, Pennsylvania	3,660	1942–2005, 2008–2011	68	4,901,000	4,880,000	2004	7,146,000	2	7,095,000
348	03031500	Allegheny River at Parker, Pennsylvania	7,671	1933–2011	79	9,991,000	10,050,000	2004	15,490,000	3	13,830,000
349	03044000	Connemaugh River at Tunnelton, Pennsylvania	1,358	1940–1991, 2010–2011	54	1,658,000	1,730,000	1951	2,519,000	5	2,150,000

Table 2. Annual runoff volumes at selected streamgages in the Central United States during water year 2011.—Continued

[mi², square miles; <, less than; >, greater than]

Map site number (fig. 4)	Station number	Station name	Contributing drainage area (mi²)	Period of record				Previous maximum annual runoff based on data through water year 2010[1]		Water year 2011	
				Water years with streamflow data	Number of years with streamflow data	Median annual runoff (acre-feet)	Mean annual runoff (acre-feet)	Water year	Annual runoff (acre-feet)	Rank	Annual runoff (acre-feet)
350	03049500	Allegheny River at Natrona, Pennsylvania	11,410	1939–2011	73	14,260,000	14,340,000	2004	21,790,000	3	19,400,000
351	03069500	Cheat River near Parsons, West Virginia	722	1914–2011	98	1,256,000	1,261,000	1996	2,266,000	19	1,477,000
352	03075070	Monongahela River at Elizabeth, Pennsylvania	5,340	1934–2011	78	6,679,000	6,693,000	1996	10,430,000	22	7,529,000
353	03086000	Ohio River at Sewickley, Pennsylvania	19,500	1934–2011	78	23,750,000	24,390,000	2004	37,210,000	7	30,990,000
356	03129000	Tuscarawas River at Newcomerstown, Ohio	2,443	1922–2011	90	1,843,000	1,900,000	2004	3,779,000	6	2,780,000
358	03140500	Muskingum River near Coshocton, Ohio	4,859	1937–2011	75	3,649,000	3,739,000	2004	6,907,000	4	5,408,000
359	03150000	Muskingum River at McConnelsville, Ohio	7,422	1922–92, 2002–2011	81	5,495,000	5,668,000	2004	9,991,000	12	7,457,000
360	03155000	Little Kanawha River at Palestine, West Virginia	1,516	1940–2011	72	1,524,000	1,556,000	1994	2,628,000	35	1,549,000
361	03159500	Hocking River at Athens, Ohio	943	1916–2011	96	722,200	746,300	2004	1,318,000	11	1,071,000
362	03176500	New River at Glen Lyn, Virginia	3,783	1928–2011	84	3,500,000	3,599,000	2003	5,423,000	43	3,497,000
363	03184000	Greenbrier River at Hilldale, West Virginia	1,619	1937–2011	75	1,651,000	1,656,000	2003	3,157,000	39	1,578,000
364	03192000	Gauley River above Belva, West Virginia	1,317	1930–2011	82	1,998,000	2,006,000	2003	2,932,000	41	2,020,000
365	03193000	Kanawha River at Kanawha Falls, West Virginia	8,371	1878–2011	134	8,977,000	9,071,000	1901	15,350,000	81	8,253,000
366	03197000	Elk River at Queen Shoals, West Virginia	1,145	1929–2011	83	1,499,000	1,493,000	1994	2,237,000	37	1,542,000
367	03198000	Kanawha River at Charleston, West Virginia	10,448	1941–2011	71	11,080,000	11,040,000	2004	16,510,000	42	10,640,000
368	03212500	Levisa Fork at Paintsville, Kentucky	2,144	1916, 1929–2011	84	1,774,000	1,786,000	1994	3,062,000	19	2,179,000
369	03213700	Tug Fork at Williamson, West Virginia	936	1968–2011	44	818,100	810,200	1979	1,252,000	26	724,000
370	03214500	Tug Fork at Kermit, West Virginia	1,280	1916–17, 1930–34, 1986–2011	33	1,057,000	1,054,000	1994	1,651,000	18	1,021,000

Table 2. Annual runoff volumes at selected streamgages in the Central United States during water year 2011.—Continued

[mi², square miles; <, less than; >, greater than]

Table 2   57

Map site number (fig. 4)	Station number	Station name	Contributing drainage area (mi²)	Period of record — Water years with streamflow data	Period of record — Number of years with streamflow data	Median annual runoff (acre-feet)	Mean annual runoff (acre-feet)	Previous maximum annual runoff based on data through water year 2010[1] — Water year	Previous maximum annual runoff based on data through water year 2010[1] — Annual runoff (acre-feet)	Water year 2011 — Rank	Water year 2011 — Annual runoff (acre-feet)
371	03227500	Scioto River at Columbus, Ohio	1,629	1921–90, 1992–2011	90	1,137,000	1,075,000	2008	1,875,000	2	1,824,000
372	03234500	Scioto River at Higby, Ohio	5,131	1931–2011	81	3,490,000	3,542,000	1996	5,937,000	4	5,531,000
373	03253500	Licking River at Catawba, Kentucky	3,300	1916–17, 1929–2011	85	2,954,000	3,015,000	1979	5,596,000	12	4,148,000
376	03274000	Great Miami River at Hamilton, Ohio	3,630	1928–2011	84	2,534,000	2,546,000	2008	4,604,000	2	4,293,000
377	03276500	Whitewater River at Brookville, Indiana	1,224	1916–17, 1924–2011	90	1,014,000	991,800	1996	1,738,000	9	1,491,000
379	03282000	Kentucky River at Lock 14 at Heidelberg, Kentucky	2,657	1926–31, 1939–2011	79	2,686,000	2,692,000	1994	5,046,000	21	3,222,000
380	03284500	Kentucky River at Lock 8 near Camp Nelson, Kentucky	4,414	1940–71, 2003–11	41	4,134,000	4,087,000	2004	6,574,000	10	5,061,000
381	03290500	Kentucky River at Lock 2 at Lockport, Kentucky	5,984	1926–30, 1933–37, 1940–2011	82	5,919,000	6,050,000	1927	10,570,000	22	7,240,000
383	03294500	Ohio River at Louisville, Kentucky	91,170	1929–2011	83	84,710,000	85,500,000	2004	133,900,000	9	110,800,000
384	03298500	Salt River at Shepherdsville, Kentucky	1,197	1939–2011	73	1,100,000	1,169,000	1979	2,621,000	13	1,586,000
386	03308500	Green River at Munfordville, Kentucky	1,493	1916–22, 1928–31, 1938–2011	85	1,984,000	1,974,000	1979	3,830,000	24	2,389,000
387	03320000	Green River at Lock 2 at Calhoun, Kentucky	6,032	1931–2011	81	8,036,000	8,080,000	1979	16,000,000	14	10,500,000
388	03325000	Wabash River at Wabash, Indiana	1,768	1924–34, 1936–2011	87	1,187,000	1,165,000	1950	2,165,000	11	1,651,000
389	03329000	Wabash River at Logansport, Indiana	3,779	1924–2011	88	2,530,000	2,564,000	1950	4,785,000	20	3,316,000
390	03336000	Wabash River at Covington, Indiana	8,218	1940–2011	72	5,596,000	5,729,000	1950	10,860,000	18	7,131,000
391	03341500	Wabash River at Terre Haute, Indiana	12,263	1928–2011	84	8,434,000	8,311,000	1950	16,510,000	16	10,430,000
392	03351000	White River near Nora, Indiana	1,219	1930–2011	82	883,300	869,300	2007	1,491,000	14	1,224,000
393	03360500	White River at Newberry, Indiana	4,688	1929–2011	83	3,757,000	3,688,000	2008	6,458,000	15	4,858,000

Table 2. Annual runoff volumes at selected streamgages in the Central United States during water year 2011.—Continued

[mi², square miles; <, less than; >, greater than]

| Map site number (fig. 4) | Station number | Station name | Contributing drainage area (mi²) | Period of record | | | Mean annual runoff (acre-feet) | Previous maximum annual runoff based on data through water year 2010[1] | | Water year 2011 | |
				Water years with streamflow data	Number of years with streamflow data	Median annual runoff (acre-feet)		Water year	Annual runoff (acre-feet)	Rank	Annual runoff (acre-feet)
394	03373500	East Fork White River at Shoals, Indiana	4,927	1904–05, 1910–16, 1924–2011	97	4,358,000	4,181,000	1950	7,529,000	9	6,154,000
395	03374000	White River at Petersburg, Indiana	11,125	1929–2011	83	9,629,000	9,171,000	1950	16,510,000	7	13,030,000
398	03376500	Patoka River near Princeton, Indiana	822	1935–2011	77	760,200	772,200	1950	1,506,000	11	1,173,000
399	03377500	Wabash River at Mount Carmel, Illinois	28,635	1928–2011	84	22,370,000	21,240,000	1950	41,050,000	11	29,320,000
402	03381500	Little Wabash River at Carmi, Illinois	3,102	1940–2011	72	2,255,000	2,081,000	1950	4,409,000	3	3,685,000
407	03404500	Cumberland River at Cumberland Falls, Kentucky	1,977	1908–11, 1916–31, 1933–94, 2003–05, 2011	86	2,349,000	2,345,000	1927	3,765,000	4	3,598,000
408	03431500	Cumberland River at Nashville, Tennessee	12,856	1893–1954, 1993–2011	81	14,330,000	14,700,000	1920	25,340,000	27	16,650,000
409	03455000	French Broad River near Newport, Tennessee	1,858	1904–05, 1921–94, 1997–2011	91	2,114,000	2,111,000	1973	3,359,000	55	1,940,000
410	03528000	Clinch River Above Tazewell, Tennessee	1,474	1920–2011	92	1,528,000	1,479,000	1927	2,367,000	35	1,614,000
411	03532000	Powell River near Arthur, Tennessee	685	1920–1981, 1997–2011	77	818,100	803,600	1974	1,347,000	24	905,000
412	03566000	Hiwassee River at Charleston, Tennessee	2,298	1901–02, 1921–39, 1964–76, 1980–81, 1988–2011	61	3,410,000	3,319,000	1990	4,988,000	51	2,317,000
413	03584600	Elk River at Prospect, Tennessee	1,805	1905–07, 1920–94, 1999–2001, 2004–2011	89	2,194,000	2,198,000	1920	3,946,000	57	2,056,000

Table 2   59

Table 2.   Annual runoff volumes at selected streamgages in the Central United States during water year 2011.—Continued

[mi², square miles; <, less than; >, greater than]

Map site number (fig. 4)	Station number	Station name	Contributing drainage area (mi²)	Period of record				Previous maximum annual runoff based on data through water year 2010[1]		Water year 2011	
				Water years with stream-flow data	Number of years with streamflow data	Median annual runoff (acre-feet)	Mean annual runoff (acre-feet)	Water year	Annual runoff (acre-feet)	Rank	Annual runoff (acre-feet)
414	03603000	Duck River above Hurricane Mills, Tennessee	2,557	1926–94, 1999–2001, 2009–11	75	2,860,000	2,966,000	1973	6,313,000	44	2,700,000
416	03611500	Ohio River at Metropolis, Illinois	203,000	1929–2011	83	201,300,000	202,100,000	1979	316,400,000	26	233,100,000
		Lower Mississippi River Basin (downstream from the mouth of the Ohio River)									
420	07026040	Obion River at Highway 51 near Obion, Tennessee	1,875	1930–58, 1967–95, 2002–11	68	1,940,000	1,995,000	1973	3,873,000	24	2,201,000
421	07030050	Hatchie River at Rialto, Tennessee	2,308	1941–74, 1977–78, 1980–84, 1986–88, 2004–11	52	2,186,000	2,333,000	1973	4,894,000	24	2,252,000
426	07032000	Mississippi River at Memphis, Tennessee	932,800	1934–2011	78	374,100,000	365,800,000	1973	571,100,000	4	515,500,000
437	07047970	Mississippi River at Helena, Arkansas	941,800	1929–2011	83	378,900,000	369,700,000	1973	589,400,000	7	511,100,000
443	07060500	White River at Calico Rock, Arkansas	9,980	1940–2011	72	7,370,000	7,430,000	1945	16,580,000	18	9,701,000
444	07061000	White River at Batesville, Arkansas	11,070	1938–58, 1987–94, 2001–11	40	9,593,000	9,157,000	1945	19,190,000	10	11,290,000
447	07064000	Black River near Corning, Arkansas	1,750	1939–95, 1999–2011	70	1,321,000	1,368,000	1973	2,903,000	11	1,998,000
448	07068000	Current River at Doniphan, Missouri	2,038	1922–2011	90	1,991,000	2,035,000	1985	4,243,000	11	2,773,000
451	07072500	Black River at Black Rock, Arkansas	7,370	1930–31, 1940–2011	74	5,814,000	6,321,000	1973	12,520,000	13	8,688,000
455	07077000	White River at DeValls Bluff, Arkansas	23,400	1950–1970, 1989–2011	44	19,870,000	19,460,000	1950	37,140,000	20	21,860,000
461	07144300	Arkansas River at Wichita, Kansas	33,227	1935–2011	77	631,300	754,900	1993	2,787,000	75	154,200
462	07151000	Salt Fork Arkansas River at Tonkawa, Oklahoma	4,470	1936–2011	76	568,700	650,800	1999	2,693,000	72	106,400

Table 2. Annual runoff volumes at selected streamgages in the Central United States during water year 2011.—Continued

[mi², square miles; <, less than; >, greater than]

Map site number (fig. 4)	Station number	Station name	Contributing drainage area (mi²)	Period of record				Previous maximum annual runoff based on data through water year 2010[1]		Water year 2011	
				Water years with streamflow data	Number of years with streamflow data	Median annual runoff (acre-feet)	Mean annual runoff (acre-feet)	Water year	Annual runoff (acre-feet)	Rank	Annual runoff (acre-feet)
463	07152000	Chikaskia River near Blackwell, Oklahoma	1,873	1937–2011	75	362,000	449,900	1999	1,441,000	71	73,850
464	07152500	Arkansas River at Ralston, Oklahoma	46,631	1926–2011	86	3,584,000	3,965,000	1999	12,160,000	84	810,900
465	07160000	Cimarron River near Guthrie, Oklahoma	12,932	1938–76, 1984–2011	67	680,500	831,100	1987	2,824,000	66	160,700
466	07164500	Arkansas River at Tulsa, Oklahoma	62,811	1926–2011	86	5,350,000	5,610,000	1999	16,580,000	86	688,500
467	07176000	Verdigris River near Claremore, Oklahoma	6,451	1936–2011	76	2,827,000	3,086,000	1999	7,891,000	62	883,300
468	07183000	Neosho River near Iola, Kansas	3,723	1896–97, 1899–1903, 1918–2011	101	1,158,000	1,365,000	1951	4,807,000	79	522,700
475	07191500	Neosho River near Chouteau, Oklahoma	11,580	1938–1950, 1964–2011	61	6,081,000	6,517,000	1993	16,070,000	42	4,959,000
486	07245000	Canadian River near Whitefield, Oklahoma	39,149	1939–2011	73	3,707,000	4,317,000	1993	11,000,000	60	1,643,000
490	07289000	Mississippi River at Vicksburg, Mississippi	1,140,500	1932–2011	80	448,100,000	443,400,000	1973	720,400,000	10	568,300,000
491	07290000	Big Black River near Bovina, Mississippi	2,812	1937–2011	75	2,592,000	2,766,000	1983	7,891,000	68	1,419,000

[1]The U.S. Geological Survey water year begins October 1 of the previous calendar year and ends September 30 of the calendar year.